Gaborabilia

Gaborabilia

ANTHONY TURTU   **DONALD F. REUTER**

Three Rivers Press • New York

dedicated to the "Gabor" in all of us

written by
Anthony Turtu and Donald F. Reuter

creative direction and design by
Donald F. Reuter and Anthony Turtu

all materials (unless otherwise noted) from the private collection of
Anthony Turtu

special still-life photography by
Billy Jim

Published by Three Rivers Press, New York, New York.
Member of the Crown Publishing Group.

Random House, Inc. New York, Toronto, London, Sydney, Auckland
www.randomhouse.com

THREE RIVERS PRESS is a registered trademark and the Three Rivers Press colophon is a trademark of Random House, Inc.

Printed in China

Library of Congress Cataloging-in-Publication Data is available upon request.

ISBN 0-609-80759-5

10 9 8 7 6 5 4 3 2 1

First Edition

frontispiece: A collage of selected Gabor memorabilia from the private collection of coauthor and "superfan" Anthony Turtu.

previous spread: Zsa Zsa Gabor to infinity and beyond! A gorgeous early sixties photograph taken from a **Coronet** magazine shoot. Amusingly, when once asked by a reporter if she ever regretted being so outspoken, Zsa Zsa shrugged, "No. They can only kill you once." (Globe)

opposite: A playful Zsa Zsa, with her poodle, Mimi. (Globe)

left: Eva Gabor graces the cover of Dutch **Actie** magazine from the mid-forties. (AC)

above: This charming perfume carousel was part of a multiple magazine promotion for a line of fragrances, including Le Couturier and Lis'n Dear, endorsed by the Gabor family in the fifties. One of our favorite pieces of "Gaborabilia." (AC)

Contents

opposite: A gorgeous publicity shot of Eva Gabor from her contract days at **Paramount Studios** during the early 1940s. (Author's collection)

left: After the release of the film *The Rescuers Down Under* (**Disney**/1990), Eva's character, Miss Bianca, became an adorable Christmas tree ornament from fast-food giant, McDonald's. (Author's collection)

above: An English edition of famed **Photoplay** magazine. One of many items of memorabilia from the 1952 film *Moulin Rouge* that featured the image of Zsa Zsa—in what is considered her best movie role—as *chanteuse* and artist Toulouse-Latrec's muse, Jane Avril. Without doubt, no one was more perfectly suited to play the part. (Author's collection)

Foreword
A Chat with
Mr. Steve Allen

Mr. Steve Allen is widely credited to have "invented" the talk show format—which for many of us was when we first became familiar with the Gabors. We were very fortunate that he agreed to let us include his wise words and wisdom in our humble project. We understand that this was one of his last official "bits of business" before his untimely passing on October 30, 2000.

We first asked the *dean* of American talk show hosts what it was about the talk show format that allowed for it to prosper—even today. His answer was succinct and direct: "There is almost nothing to it. In other words, it simply boils down to sixty minutes of whatever people want to do to fill up the space, so long as it involves, predominately, interviews or casual conversations." Rather surprisingly, he added that, "talent on the part of the host was by no means a requirement." However, he did point out that what a person did for a living *prior* to becoming a host would have some bearing on their success. Mr. Allen was himself a professional comedian. He also noted that the success of a talk show, "depended heavily on the talent or charm of their guests," but unless a given guest does a comedy performance or a musical number "the guest doesn't have to be talented, either." How true! However, he did interject that what a guest *does* have to be is a "good conversationalist" or rather that they have "a gift for casual conversation"—and it would be helpful if they had some kind of "sparkle."

Which brings us to the Gabors—and why they were so perfect for the medium. Zsa Zsa, he said in particular, was "a great chatterer" and had "a *cute* sense of humor." Cute? Unfortunately, we were not able to clarify why he chose to describe Ms. Gabor's wit in such a way. One could surmise that he was just being diplomatic when selecting his words. He also remarked that it was quite relevant to any discussion of their celebrity that Zsa Zsa possessed "one of the most beautiful faces in the history of—well, faces." We also asked if he felt there was anyone quite like the Gabors today. To this he replied, "I don't believe there is anyone like them today. There is also nobody around today like Jimmy Cagney, Edward G. Robinson, Clark Gable, Greta Garbo, W.C. Fields, Groucho Marx, Mae West, and scores of other names that could be mentioned."

We also queried him on his own personal observations of the Gabors—*behind the scenes*. Interestingly, he felt that Eva marketed herself—"and darling merchandise it was"—largely as a derivation of Zsa Zsa's personality and appearance. Because his own wife, Jayne Meadows, and sister, Audrey, were inextricably linked in much the same manner, his take is well supported. This was not a criticism of Eva—with whom he had a longstanding and "pleasant" relationship—but he believed his thoughts might seem odd to people who were much more familiar with Eva, especially because of *Green Acres*, than they ever were of Zsa Zsa's work.

Last, he said that one of the rarer qualities the Gabors had was *glamour*. Which, by the time they came on the scene in the fifties, was already in "short supply" and "that happy fact enabled them to stand out" among the crowd. To have natural glamour, he added, "is something that cannot be learned. Either you have it or you don't—and very few people do. Being pretty or even strikingly beautiful has almost nothing to do with it."

above: Hello Dalí! Eva Gabor joins television legend Steve Allen on his first talk show for CBS in 1951. In this still, "Steverino" and cohost Eva interview the enigmatic surrealist painter Salvador Dalí, live on the steps of St. Patrick's Cathedral in New York City. It was the first of numerous times that Mr. Allen would play host to one or all the the Gabor sisters. Thanks to the talk show format that he pioneered, Mr. Allen was instrumental in bringing the glamour and humor of the Gabor family into living rooms across the country. (Corbis)

Jolie Gàbor, Inc.
EXCLUSIVE JEWELRY
699 MADISON AVENUE
New York, N. Y. 10021   July 8, 1978

To Tony Turtu

Dear Tony,

Thank you for your letter. I am so delighted
that you enjoyed my book and also that you are a fan of
mine , when I have such beautiful daughters to compeat
with.   Letter,s like yours help make my day.

Best Wishes
Jolie
Jolie

I was ten years old when I first caught a glimpse of one of *them*. As I sat cross-legged on the living room floor, finishing the next day's homework assignment, Merv Griffin introduced Zsa Zsa on his syndicated talk show. I had never seen anything quite like Zsa Zsa before, and I became immediately fascinated by the pretty lady with the funny name and the even funnier accent. With her blindingly blonde coiffure and dangerously long eyelashes, she seemed to me to be almost otherwordly. It was as if she lived in the flash of color, or in the sparkle of a jewel. Whatever it was—I was hooked!

To my surprise, I later discovered that there were two more sisters and a glamorous mother who made up this legendary family. The entire clan appeared on talk shows—*all* talk shows! Unshakable, they held their own against feminists and rival glamour gals without seeming to ruffle an ostrich feather. No topic could render them speechless and I would secretly feel sorry for any guest who had to follow a "Gabor." As I grew up, I came to enjoy their work on episodic television, scanning the *TV Guide* in advance so as to highlight any Gabor sightings for the following week.

At fifteen, I nervously rang the doorbell at Jolie Gabor's chic Madison Avenue jewelry shop in New York City, and with my allowance money, purchased her newly published memoirs, *Jolie Gabor*, which were displayed in the front windows amid pictures of her famous daughters. After college, I started collecting memorabilia which featured these alluring ladies. Most dealers were delighted by my hobby (though some haughtily feigned indifference) and would call me with the news of a movie poster for Zsa Zsa or a magazine with Eva on its cover.

This collection has grown to almost epic proportions

Preface

opposite: A starstruck teen marks a major early milestone in his collecting of "Gaborabilia." Upon writing to the family matriarch, Jolie, at her Palm Springs residence in the mid-seventies, coauthor Anthony Turtu receives back this charming reply—accompanied by a small autographed postcard. In this picture, the prized items are also accompanied by a business card used to promote the jewelry salon.

above: One of *über*-collector Anthony Turtu's most cherished pieces of memorabilia is this original and hard-to-find title card from *Love Island* (**Astor**/ 1949). This extremely low-budget epic cast Eva Gabor as Sarna, a tropical temptress whose long dark wig did nothing to mask a pronounced Hungarian accent! (Author's collection)

LIBERTY

Canada's young family magazine

10 cents
March, 1960

JACQUES PLANTE:
The torment of goalies

Do Canadians take pride in race prejudice?

B.C.'s fantastic women

Does TV harm children?

How to spot hidden troubles in marriage

Why I tried suicide

Our credit card craze

by FABIAN
I sing without trying

by ZSA ZSA GABOR
My life is never dull

As surely as collectibles can delight the collector, they can also frustrate, as is the case with these two incorrectly identified pieces of paper ephemera. *above:* Though Zsa Zsa Gabor is given title credit, the actual cover girl for **Liberty**, a Canadian magazine from March 1960, is sister Eva. *right:* A 1958 British arcade card promoting Eva's romantic comedy *The Truth About Women* is mistakenly illustrated with a portrait of Zsa Zsa. Being constantly confused with each other was said to have driven the sisters crazy—to say nothing of their fans! (Author's collection)

opposite: With the Hollywood Hills a fitting backdrop, Zsa Zsa strikes a glamorous pose in an elegant sixties couture gown. (Sid Avery/MPTV)

and became the basis for this book. It also serves as a reminder that we will never see a phenomenon quite like the Gabors ever again. They survived (and prospered) in the fickle and often heartbreaking world of celebrity for five decades, and though they have occasionally fallen out of favor with the public, they have nonetheless pierced the very core of international pop culture and will no doubt remain there.

Here's looking at you, girls…

Anthony Turtu

What are my first recollections of the Gabors? Visions of silly, beautiful, slightly troublesome women; like shiny, but bad pennies that kept turning up. The time is the mid-seventies, and even as a youngster I sensed that they were hucksters, selling me something that I didn't need but bought anyway. They made me laugh, too, though I was never sure with them or at them.

Like many others, my impressions of Zsa Zsa, Eva, (vaguely) Magda, and momma Jolie were influenced by their celebrity which had, by that time, long eclipsed any sense of who they really were. Many years later, after happening upon my good friend Tony's immense collection of Gabor "lore," I found myself greatly interested in getting to know them better—and understanding how they became such popular cultural icons. (It didn't hurt that at the same time my Korean mother was reading a years-old copy of one of Zsa Zsa's two autobiographies, either!)

This humble effort—a visual gift to their "legacy"—is an attempt to show the Gabors in a more flattering light than they have been afforded over most of their lifetime. I certainly came to realize their careers were far more substantial than I had been led to believe and am reminded that not too long ago the Gabor women were considered among the most beautiful in the world. Though they may be percieved as nothing more than sugary frosting, the reality is that the Gabors' "success" was based on more than just empty calories; they made the most of what they had to work with. Let's all eat cake!

13

In za Beginning

B y now, the story of the Gabor family and their entrance and assimilation into the public spotlight is quite well known. However, it is the early years of this glittering dynasty that sometimes gets glossed over, if mentioned at all. The fascinating tale of their early lives reads like a cross between *Doctor Zhivago* and *Gypsy*, with a generous helping of *Fiddler on the Roof* and *Auntie Mame* thrown in for good measure.

Jolie, the beautiful *queen* of the Gabor clan, was born Jansci Tilleman, the third child of Francesca and Josef Tilleman, around the turn of the century. Her mother, the former Francesca Reinherz, was born in Vienna and married Josef, a struggling university student, eloping to Budapest with him. Early in their marriage the newlyweds invested every cent they had in a small luncheonette, where Josef and Francesca sometimes worked eighteen hours a day. With their keen business sense the tiny restaurant became quite profitable and Francesca turned her attention to much greener pastures. Her parents owned a chain of jewelry shops in Austria, and with a relatives help, the young bride opened The Diamond House, which she and Josef turned into one of the most fashionable and successful boutiques in Hungary.

When Jolie was born, the Tillemans were already proud parents of two other daughters, Janette and Dora. After Jolie came another sister, Rosalie, and then a son, Sebastyn (or Sebi, as he was called), who became the apple of Francesca's eye. (Many years later, in a tragic and darker moment in Jolie's life, both Sebi and her beloved mother, Francesca, were killed in a bombing raid while inside the Portuguese legation center in Hungary during World War II.)

As a young girl, Jolie had aspirations of becoming an actress and pursued her dream with all the drive and determination she would later use on her own daughters. It was, however, a different time and place, and a career on the "wicked stage" was unthinkable for young girls from respectable families like Jolie's. If she was to become a sensation in the theatre, she would have to find another way. A handsome army major and businessman named Vilmos Gabor just might be the ticket, and Jolie's plan (which would rival anything that Lucy Ricardo could concieve) was put into place.

The dashing and distinguished Vilmos was so captivated with the seventeen-year-old Jolie that he agreed to marry her, and if her burning desire to become an actress wasn't dimmed in six months, he would grant her a divorce. This way she would be free to pursue her dream as a "fallen woman"! With social conventions as they were it just wouldn't have been proper for a fine young lady to become an actress, but it would be perfectly acceptable for a "scandalous divorcée" to do so. However, little Magda Gabor's birth delayed Jolie's plan, as did Zsa Zsa's (born Sari) and finally Eva's—all within the first four years of marriage. Motherhood squelched Jolie's desire to strut upon the stage, instead becoming the "behind-the-scenes" director for the fate of these three little girls who looked to her for love and support.

As children each Gabor daughter would take tennis and riding lessons, ballet and figure skating, study languages, and were exposed to the theatre and opera world early on in their young lives. Zsa Zsa even went on to become a Junior Fencing Champion in Budapest! If her own personal aspirations were sidelined, Jolie's dreams for her daughters had only just begun. Her efforts were successful beyond any expectation, perhaps even her own. By the late 1930s each Gabor sister (though still only teenagers) was married and safely away from the ever-impending threat of war which engulfed Europe at the time. Zsa Zsa was the wife of Burhan Belge, the press director for the Foreign Ministry of Turkey in Ankara; Eva, hoping for an acting career (as her mother had), married Dr. Eric Drimmer, a Swedish osteopath, and briefly moved to London with him before settling in Hollywood where she tried her luck in motion pictures; and Magda, who married a Polish count and RFA fighter pilot named Jan de Bichovsky, staying a little closer to home in Warsaw. Through Jolie's imaginative choreography, these

opposite: A newly arrived "Sari" Gabor, taken in 1941. Originally, Zsa Zsa was named after famed Hungarian actress Sari Fedak, one of starstruck Jolie Gabor's idols. The name "Zsa Zsa" was actually a moniker given to *La Fedak* by her own baby daughter. Our Zsa Zsa also took the nickname for herself, and made it world famous. Incidentally, our young émigré was said to have lunched at famed restaurant "21" a mere three hours after arriving in New York City. Way to go! (MPTV)

above: Publicity still. Eva, the first of the three Gabor sisters to emigrate to the United States, fulfilled a childhood dream of becoming an actress by quickly signing a contract with **Paramount Studios.** Unfortunately, Eva seemed to have spent more of her time in front of the still camera and less on the movie screen. Sadly, the studio dropped her after only two starring roles. (Author's collection)

lovely ladies grew into stunning women who captivated the world on the grandest scale for more than fifty years.

Interestingly, it wasn't until Jolie divorced Vilmos and later set out for America (arriving on New Year's Eve, 1945) that she too experienced the kind of fame she had always dreamed of for herself. Opening the Jolie Gabor Pearl Salon shortly after her arrival, continuing the retail and design tradition which started with her grandparents so many years before, she became the toast of New York. She was also able to share the same kind of success and independence now being enjoyed by her three most dazzling creations: Magda, Zsa Zsa, and Eva Gabor.

For the next half century, this Magyar mother hen would rule supreme over her trio of beautiful chicks. With her own fame she would not only oversee a business empire but still find time to maintain her position as the "queen" of New York and Palm Springs café society—with her devoted third husband, Edmund de Szigethy, at her side. Her glamourous reign lasted until her death in 1997.

opposite: Eva and Magda help middle sister Zsa Zsa celebrate another birthday—we're *not* saying which one—at celebrity watering hole The Stork Club, in the early sixties. Wouldn't you just die to know what she wished for!? (Corbis)

left: Zsa Zsa and her daughter Francesca Hilton (from her marriage to hotelier Conrad Hilton) share a lovely moment swimming together during a Monte Carlo vacation in 1964—which obviously did not go unnoticed by the European paparazzi and **Hola!** magazine. Zsa Zsa returned many times to the jet-set beaches of Europe since the early 1950s, and even narrated a television travelogue about the Riviera for NBC in 1961. (Author's collection)

above: A radiant Zsa Zsa kisses her mother, Jolie, goodbye at Idlewild Airport (1954). Zsa Zsa was *en route* to the film festival at Cannes, but hinted that she might rendezvous with her then lover, Dominican diplomat Porfirio Rubirosa, in Paris. (Corbis)

21

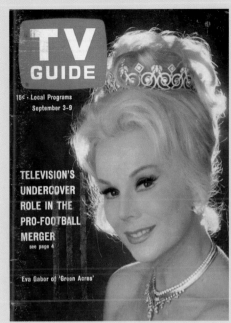

Zat's Entertainment

"'Forced Landing' was a B-picture only to those too lazy to go down the alphabet."

—Eva Gabor, with her thoughts on her first starring role

From the very beginning, Hollywood has been home to dynasty after dynasty of celebrated acting families. Their names read like a who's who of entertainment royalty. Among them, the Barrymores, the Fondas, the Bridgeses, Fontaine and DeHavilland, Beatty and MacLaine, and the list goes on. Would it be so difficult to include the Gabors into this rarefied group? Certainly, if sheer longevity, countless credits, and unbridled fame is our barometer, then hands down, they move straight to the top of the list. However, if critical acclaim and accolades are our criteria, then maybe not. Which seems unfair, given the skewed quality standards we often use to judge a body of work. Even more so, knowing that they did appear in some very excellent work and performed, at times, as well as could be expected, considering the often marginal material they were given. Undoubtedly, during the early to mid-fifties, when all three—Eva, Zsa Zsa, and Magda—were at the peak of their notoriety, they must have been a perfumed and powdered force to be reckoned with. Moreover, if Zsa Zsa had kept her career on track following an interesting (and most credible) acting turn in *Moulin Rouge* (United Artists/1952) directed by John Huston, we would have been treated to a vastly different body of work. Eva, too, proven to be a very fine comedienne, had her own problems in this regard. It was not until "Green Acres" that she would attain any longlasting praise for her talents. However, it may have been more the shameful stereotyping inherent in many women's roles so rampant in those days which made it all too diffi-

above: Publicity still from *A Royal Scandal* (**20th Century Fox**/1945), featuring Eva in a small role as the Countess Demidow. Oddly, the original director, Ernst Lubitsch, was replaced by Otto Preminger, who completed the picture. This gave Eva the chance to work for two of Hollywood's greatest filmmakers in one movie. The film is also a rare opportunity to see the indominatible Tallulah Bankhead playing the role of Catherine the Great. (Photofest).

right: A screen still from the low-budget swash-buckler, *The Wife of Monte Cristo* (**Producers Releasing Corporation**/1946). Shown from left to right are stars Leonore Aubert, John Loder, and Eva Gabor. At this point in her movie career, appearing in B-minus films such as this one was, sadly, the only work that young ingenue Eva could find. Fortunately, during this period she was wed to her second husband, millionaire Charles Isaacs—who allowed Eva to struggle in comfort! (Author's collection)

cult for them (and many others) to properly develop their careers. But we don't have to cry for the Gabors; their legend is secure. Given the circumstances, they managed to fashion for themselves an impressively long resume of credits, if not a consistently sterling one.

Eva, the youngest, was also the first to be "bitten" by the acting bug. (Although it must be noted that momma Jolie, herself, had always wanted to be an actress—but found it an illusive dream.) Having moved to Hollywood, via London, in the late thirties, with then-husband, osteopath Dr. Erik Drimmer, Eva immediately set upon the studios in search of work. Paramount was the first studio to take the bait and immediately began grooming their neophyte starlet—whom some had prematurely pegged as the next "Garbo." Unfortunately Eva, then only in her late teens, photographed even younger, making her extremely difficult to cast. Despite early promise, she would flounder for the next ten years, appearing in one forgettable film after another until she finally landed successfully in 1950 on Broadway, in the Rodgers and Hammerstein production of *The Happy Time.* Seemingly, to make up for those lost years, her workload was not limited to the stage. She hosted a self-titled radio show and two television programs: "The Eva Gabor

opposite: Lobby card detail. Casting a petite, blonde starlet with a Hungarian accent as a raven-haired South Sea temptress in **Astor Pictures'** *Love Island* (1949) may have seemed like a good idea to producer Sol Loesser at the time, but the result was a disaster and the film quickly disappeared from theatres. Fortunately for Eva, shown here with costar Paul Valentine, great success on the Broadway stage was less than a year away, and she, understandably, never mentioned this clinker in any future bios or interviews. (Ironically, the film was rereleased in 1953—obviously hoping to capitalize on its star's newfound fame—but it still failed to set box offices ablaze.) (Author's collection)

below: Publicity still detail. As the glamorous Countess Marina, Eva appeared opposite Claude Rains and Wanda Hendrix in the romantic 1949 costume-drama, *Song of Surrender,* directed by Mitchell Leisen for **Paramount Pictures**. (Author's collection)

top: Lobby card. *Lovely to Look At* (**MGM**/1954) was the lavish remake of the Astaire-Rogers classic musical, *Roberta* (*RKO*/1935) and marked Zsa Zsa's film debut. Here she is surrounded by costars Ann Miller, Kurt Kasznar, Kathryn Grayson, Howard Keel, Marge and Gower Champion, and Red Skelton. (Author's collection)

above: Halfsheet poster. *Paris Model* (**Columbia**/ 1954) was a low-budget anthology that followed four women who each buy a copy of the same "nude at midnight" gown. Eva played "Gogo" in one vignette, a role originally intended for Zsa Zsa. (Author's collection)

right: Original Spanish lobby card from Zsa Zsa's first foreign film, *El Enemigo Publico No. 1* (1953), where she played seductive gun moll Lola with top-billed French comedian Fernandel. (Author's collection)

opposite: Lobby card detail. *We're Not Married* (**Fox**/1952) was a charming comedy directed by Edmund Goulding. In one of five episodes, Zsa Zsa costars as a scheming fortune hunter—with very few lines of dialogue—opposite Louis Calhern. (Author's collection)

Show" and "Famous Women of History." This resurrection of her career came at a time when it was most needed. But the celebration would be short-lived; for on the horizon loomed Zsa Zsa, inching ever closer to the cameras.

Zsa Zsa made an early attempt at acting when she very young, as the heroine, Violetta, in the Viennese operetta *The Singing Dream*. But her personal life quickly overshadowed any blossoming career, remaining away from the footlights for all the forties. It wasn't until her marriage to actor George Sanders in 1949 that Zsa Zsa was even in the position to *reconsider* becoming an actress. In fact, it was rather accidental that she became one at all. The story of how it happened is the Gabor-version of *A Star Is Born*.

About the same time that Eva was conquering the East Coast on Broadway, Zsa Zsa was enjoying life with the acclaimed Hollywood thespian. However, the five-year marriage to George Sanders would be anything but idyllic. Notwithstanding the claim by Zsa Zsa that George would be "the love of her life," it could not have been a very fulfilling union. It seemed George had the habit of leaving his wife alone for very long periods of time, often while he was away filming on location. Any attempts by her to accompany him were frequently met with disdain. So, it was during one of these all-too-familiar disappearances that Zsa Zsa was called upon by George's

ZSA-ZSA GABOR

above: Zsa Zsa shares the cover of this regional television magazine, **American T-Vue Time**, with legendary funnyman, Jack Benny. Ironically, the unusual pairing of Zsa Zsa and Benny was for a dramatic **General Electric** teleplay, "The Honest Man." However, Zsa Zsa was well acquainted with Mr. Benny's brand of memorable humor, already having guest starred on his successful self-titled comedy show. (Author's collection)

right: Television guide. A beautiful color photo of Eva adorns the cover of **TV Show** magazine (March 1952). By this time, Eva had carved out an impressive career on the "small screen," with countless guest spots and two shows of her own including "Famous Women of History." As the title suggests, Eva portrayed a different legendary female each week. (Author's collection)

opposite: Though divorced two years earlier, Zsa Zsa starred opposite ex-husband George Sanders in the **Ford Theatre** tele-drama "Autumn Fever" (1956) as the beautiful Dara Szabo. (Author's collection)

brother, Tom Conway (also an actor), to help out in a professional crisis. Tom, who was on his way to a taping of "Bachelor's Haven"—a popular West Coast panel show at the time—asked Zsa Zsa to come along and fill a last-minute vacancy on the dais. Reluctantly, she agreed, more it seemed to secretly get back at her husband, who had alluded that she "had no talent." Her misgivings were short-lived; by the time she appeared on camera in a beautiful, black Balenciaga dress dusted with diamonds (her own), it was clear that the camera adored her. What came out of her mouth, unrehearsed, was pure Gabor. Answering one letter in particular, live on the air, when asked how to deal with a husband who was a traveling salesman—and possibly unfaithful—Zsa Zsa advised a listener to "shoot him in the legs." She was an immediate success and the producers clamored to have her back. Furthermore, the legend continues, famed director/producer Mervyn LeRoy caught her "act" and was taken aback by her luminous presence. Since she didn't have an agent, he was unable to reach her at the time. However, upon spotting her at the famed Mocambo's nightclub a few days later, he sidled over to the table where she was holding court and offered her a coveted role in MGM's newest musical, *Lovely to Look At*, right there on the spot. Her career was thus launched.

If you are fortunate enough to see Zsa Zsa in some of her early work for MGM (or in *Moulin Rouge* for United Artists) you can't help but be struck by how indescribably

30 BIG FEATURES ★ PROGRAM LISTINGS

TV SHOW *March* 25¢

TV IN HOLLYWOOD

Articles By: FRANK SINATRA ★ DINAH SHORE
SAM LEVENSON ★ PETER LIND HAYES ★ GARRY MOORE

Eva Gabor

beautiful she was at the time. It has been said a person can "glow" before the cameras; if that's true, then Zsa Zsa produced quite a flame. Sadly, and for whatever reasons (many of which have been stated here and elsewhere), she was not able to keep the momentum going and soon her career veered wildly off-course. Fortunately, we have films such as *Lovely to Look At, We're Not Married, The Story of Three Loves,* and *Lili* to remind us of what all the brouhaha was about.

It was a couple of years into Zsa Zsa's career when her work became intertwined with that of sister Eva. How awkward it must have been to find your only competition for a role to be your own sibling. Just how many Hungarian-accented roles could there be to go around, even under the best of circumstances? Amusingly, they would each appear in their "own" Martin and Lewis comedy. Where each would do something of special note—Zsa Zsa in *Lili* and Eva in *The Last Time I Saw Paris*—they would invariably misstep with a less than remarkable turn in something unremarkable like *The Most Wanted Man* or *The Mad Magician*. However, noticeable distinctions between the two women's careers began to surface; Eva managed to develop a very good sense of comedy, which would obviously come in handy some years later, and she probably had the upper hand in terms of the quality of her work. A notable example: her captivating appearance as delightfully self-centered and suicidal Liane d'Exelmans in MGM's *Gigi*, the Oscar-winning Best

top right: One-sheet poster. F. Scott Fitzgerald's short story "Babylon Revisited" was adapted for the big screen and released as *The Last Time I Saw Paris* (**MGM**/1954), with Elizabeth Taylor and Van Johnson in the leads. The romantic drama about American expatriates featured strong supporting performances from Walter Pidgeon, Donna Reed, and Eva Gabor as a cynical, much-married, international globetrotter. (Author's collection)

bottom right: Illustrated movie program for the sumptuous German film *Ball der Nationen* (**Panorama**/1955). As the luscious Vera Van Loon, Zsa Zsa played opposite popular European leading man Gustav Fröhlich. (Author's collection)

far right: Leslie Caron, playing the cherubic title role of *Lili* (**MGM**/1953), is confronted by worldly Rosalie (Zsa Zsa), with onlookers Mel Ferrer, Kurt Kasznar, and Alex Gerry, in this lobby card detail. (Author's collection)

Zsa Zsa's role in *Lili* was the type of part she was perfect at playing. Always beautiful, worldly, witty, and just a touch self-important (just a touch!), these characters, though often onscreen for only short amounts of time, captivated moviegoers. However, with the completion of her charming role in *Lili* and the Martin and Lewis comedy *3 Ring Circus*, Zsa Zsa began to spend more and more time abroad— often with the new man in her life, Porfirio Rubirosa. Their romance was played out in gossip columns and chic nightclubs across Europe, ensuring Zsa Zsa's place as tabloid royalty. Not surprisingly, she never wanted for publicity for the duration of her love affair with Rubi. Unfortunately, it did keep her away from Hollywood, where she was obviously very much in demand. Sadly, in the world of motion pictures, absence *does not* make the heart grow fonder, and with the exception of a cameo role in Orson Welles's *Touch of Evil* (**Universal**/1958), Zsa Zsa doesn't appear in a major American motion picture for the remainder of the decade. She did, however, wisely reinvent herself as an actress on television—even garnering an Emmy nomination for her stint on "Bachelor's Haven"—and as a sparkling guest on talk and variety programs. Zsa Zsa's foray into television greatly extended her career further than a lot of her contemporaries, who found their professional lives in limbo following the demise of the studio system. This proved to be a brilliant strategy, as Zsa Zsa successfully continued to alternate between all mediums with great regularity for years.

36

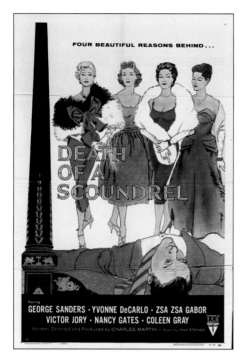

FOUR BEAUTIFUL REASONS BEHIND...

DEATH OF A SCOUNDREL

Starring
GEORGE SANDERS · YVONNE DeCARLO · ZSA ZSA GABOR
VICTOR JORY · NANCY GATES · COLEEN GRAY
Written, Directed and Produced by CHARLES MARTIN · Music by MAX STEINER

above: One-sheet poster. Though already divorced by this time, Zsa Zsa teamed with ex-hubby George Sanders in the "noir-ish" film, *Death of a Scoundrel* (**RKO**/1956), about a suave con man and the succession of "dames" who help him get ahead.
right: Lobby card. Sharing the screen with popular duo Martin and Lewis, Zsa Zsa vies with costar Joanne Dru for Dean's affections, ultimately losing him in *3 Ring Circus* (**Paramount**/1954). (Author's collection)

opposite: Detail of French film program. French heartthrob Daniel Gelin and Zsa Zsa, from *Sang et Lumieres* (**Sirius**/1954), which was successfully re-released in America under the title *Love in a Hot Climate*, in 1958, and again in 1966 as *Beauty and the Bullfighter*. (Author's collection)

Picture of 1958. Zsa Zsa, meanwhile, bounced like a human pinball from domestic films to foreign fare, nightclubs, radio, and especially television, where she worked with *everyone* from Frank Sinatra to Martha Raye and Ernie Kovacs, and on *everything*, including "Playhouse 90," "What's My Line?," and "Love That Bob."

By 1958, the year of *Gigi* and Zsa Zsa's *Queen of Outer Space*, the differences in both sisters' personalities was also quite evident. Eva took on more demure characteristics, while Zsa Zsa became ever more "larger-than-life," creating the persona which would very soon eclipse its own creator.

By the sixties, as film work waned, other avenues opened up. It is within this decade that Zsa Zsa seemed to grow even more famous, as has been quoted, "for just being famous." Certainly her career bears this through, as much of her work fell into the category of "guest star," beginning with a cameo in *Pepe* (Columbia/1960), through spots on "Bonanza" and "Gilligan's Island," among many, many others. Occasionally, she did land meatier roles, like the one for *Picture Mommy Dead*. Fortuitously, Eva stayed closer to her acting roots and interspersed roles in mild comedies such as *New Kind of Love* with summer stock and more Broadway, most notably as Vivien Leigh's replacement in the musical *Tovarich*. She kept her career afloat just long enough to land the role that would make a her a true star and finally pull her out from

A Vegas Vignette

Las Vegas, that little jewel in the desert, has played host to gamblers, gangsters, and glamour girls since its "golden age" during the fifties and sixties; a time when almost every major Hollywood star tried their hand at a successful nightclub career. Such staggeringly diverse talent as Marlene Dietrich, Mae West, Ginger Rogers, Debbie Reynolds, and Tallulah Bankhead commanded lucrative paydays for filling main showrooms. When film studios drastically cut production on the lavish spectacles many of these women had become famous for, Vegas took up the slack with its own brand of glitzy showcases. Not surprisingly, it was into this exciting milieu we would find the Gabors.

By the time the Gabor sisters appeared together in the winter of 1953 at the Last Frontier Hotel, all three were seasoned newsmakers, which only added to the already circus-like atmosphere. For their routine, they wore lavish sequined gowns of different colors as they recited witty repartee standing in front of all pink, heart-shaped podiums. The act was delightfully campy and a huge success. Even so, Zsa Zsa was the only sister to regularly return to the strip; Eva preferred legitimate theatre and Magda gave up show business in favor of the life of a socialite.

Recently, Zsa Zsa appeared at the Vegas World Hotel; when discussing her act and what fans could look forward to, Zsa Zsa joked, "Don't expect me to sing; don't expect me to do anything, and then you'll be happy."

above: Original postcard advertising one of Zsa Zsa's many appearances at the Riviera Hotel. (AC)
right: At the start of her nightclub career Zsa Zsa commanded as much as $7,500 a week and traded on her own sexy image in an act specifically tailored for her entitled "Professor of Love." (Photofest)
opposite: The three Gabors at their 1953 debut as a sister act at the Last Frontier Hotel. (Corbis)

behind Zsa Zsa's grand shadow, that being Lisa Douglas on "Green Acres." What started out as a role intended, if one can imagine, for actress Martha Hyer, became a windfall for Eva. Prior to starring in this pastoral pastiche (one of a group of inter-related CBS comedies), Eva hadn't enjoyed the success that was so anxiously anticipated with her Broadway debut, some fifteen years earlier. Not that she hadn't tried, either. It's just that real fame, separate from her magnetic sister, Zsa Zsa, would prove a somewhat illusive goal. However, upon landing the role of Lisa Douglas, Eva combined her own glamorous inclinations with a zany daffiness that would endear her to television audiences. (No small feat considering in real life she was the intellectual opposite of her small screen incarnation.) Paired perfectly with costar Eddie Albert, Eva created a character that would be one for the television history books. Hotscakes, anyone?

Interestingly, once this happened, Eva, like her sister, began showing up on many a variety, comedy, and talk show, due to her new visibility and popularity. However, it would be Zsa Zsa's early stints on the "Jack Paar Show" that forever cemented the Gabor family's reputation as the quintessential talk show guests. For forty years the talk show format would be Zsa Zsa's professional "home," and she continued to be a sparkling, witty, and, sometimes, exacerbating guest. Unwitting hosts who weren't on their toes ran the risk of throwing "the cat among the pigeons" when Zsa Zsa was turned loose. It comes as no

43

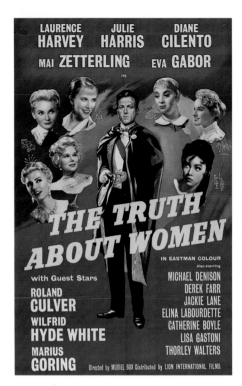

LAURENCE **HARVEY**   JULIE **HARRIS**   DIANE **CILENTO**
MAI **ZETTERLING**   EVA **GABOR**

IN

THE TRUTH ABOUT WOMEN

IN EASTMAN COLOUR

with Guest Stars

ROLAND **CULVER**

WILFRID **HYDE WHITE**

MARIUS **GORING**

MICHAEL DENISON
DEREK FARR
JACKIE LANE
ELINA LABOURDETTE
CATHERINE BOYLE
LISA GASTONI
THORLEY WALTERS

Directed by MURIEL BOX Distributed by LION INTERNATIONAL FILMS

above: British one-sheet poster. *The Truth About Women* (**Continental**/1958) was a well-mounted comedy that starred Laurence Harvey playing opposite a bevy of international beauties, including Mai Zetterling, Diane Cilento, and Eva Gabor. (AC)
right: Lobby card from *Gigi* (**MGM**/1958), easily the best film that Eva ever appeared in. As Liane d'Exelmans, she played the coquettish, sometime lover of Gaston Lachaille (Louis Jourdan), and in the process ended up costarring in the Oscar-winning Best Picture of that year. (Author's collection)

opposite: Italian one-sheet poster detail. Considered by many as a "camp" masterpiece, *The Queen of Outer Space* (**Allied Artists**/1958) starred Zsa Zsa, not as the evil monarch in the title, but as a savior to the unwitting astronauts who found themselves marooned on a planet populated only by beautiful "Venusian" glamour girls. Writer Ben Hecht, who penned *The Front Page* with Charles MacArthur, was responsible for the screenplay. Recently, when queried about the film, Zsa Zsa joked that the only direction she was given during production was to "not laugh at the dialogue." She didn't, but loyal fans found it hard not too, especially in anticipation of her immortal line, "I hate zat evil qveen!" (Author's collection)

small coincidence that many of us (authors included) first became aware of Zsa Zsa's presence upon seeing her on "Johnny," "Mike," "Merv," or "Dinah."

The seventies were not great times for any glamorous Hollywood star. The recession made the innocent ostentation of many luminaries from the "golden age" seem almost vulgar in comparison to the laidback luxe of the new regime. But you couldn't keep our gals down. Fame on the scale of a Gabor would always prove a priceless commodity. Zsa Zsa on Broadway in 1970 is the perfect case in point. Zsa Zsa on Broadway? Well, as unthinkable as the notion may be to some, to producer David Merrick it proved to be a wise, albeit unusual, choice to make. Originally, Zsa Zsa suggested that she would be perfect for the lead in Merrick's *Hello, Dolly!*, instead she found herself offered the lead in another one of his hit productions. The platinum-headed star was signed on to replace Julie Harris in the role of Anne Stanley—changed to "Anna" to make the character more continental—in his comedy smash *Forty Carats*. So successful was this collaboration that she took the show on a national tour. Other stage roles were to follow, including what must have been a very memorable night in the theatre, when she was joined by equally glam sister Eva in a revival of *Arsenic and Old Lace* in 1975, at the Arlington Park Playhouse in Chicago.

By the eighties and into the nineties, at a time when other stars might have

44

1958 was a banner year for Zsa Zsa. Her appearances in *Touch of Evil* (**Universal**/1958) and *Queen of Outer Space* were significant indicators of the power of her celebrity—though each work was wildly disparate from the other in terms of context and quality. That year, she also recieved a Golden Globe award—presented to her by none other than Alfred Hitchcock—as "1957's Most Glamorous Star." Is there any doubt she deserved *that* accolade at least once in her lifetime?

left: A behind-the-scenes still of Zsa Zsa rehearsing with director/star Orson Welles, on the set of *Touch of Evil.* Though her role consisted of a mere two lines at the film's beginning, it was still quite an "ostrich feather in her cap" to be associated with what is considered by many to be one of the greatest "film noirs" ever made. (Everett)

above: Italian movie poster. Though Zsa Zsa is not pictured on any of the American poster art for *Evil,* her enormous popularity in Europe made it essential that she be featured as prominently as her costars, Welles, Charlton Heston, Janet Leigh, and Marlene Dietrich. (Author's collection)

47

top: Lobby card. A film oddity, *Country Music Holiday* (**Paramount**/1958) featured gangsters, prizefighters, rockabilly tunes—and Zsa Zsa Gabor! Who could ask for more? (Author's collection)

above: Lobby card. *For the First Time* (**MGM**/1959) was Mario Lanza's last film. He played an opera star who befriends and falls in love with a beautiful deaf girl. Zsa Zsa portrayed Gloria de Vadnuz, a fun-loving Riviera playgirl. (Author's collection)

right: Half-sheet poster. Cantinflas (Mexico's answer to Charlie Chaplin) was the focus and title character of *Pepe* (**Columbia**/1960). Typical of the cameo-packed films of this period, Zsa Zsa found herself in a smorgasbord of famous names, including Frank Sinatra, Judy Garland, Kim Novak, Jimmy Durante, and Bing Crosby. (Author's collection)

opposite: Lobby card detail. *It Started With a Kiss* (MGM/1959) costarred Eva and her *Don't Go Near the Water* leading man, Glenn Ford. The lightweight comedy, about mistaken identity and marital infidelity, also starred Debbie Reynolds and was filmed amidst lush Spanish locales. (Author's collection)

shown signs of slowing down, both sisters continued working and plying their trade. Eva even managed a run at another television series, the short-lived "Bridges to Cross" on CBS (in 1985). She continued doing episodic television, filming her own pilot for another series, and costarring in the made-for-TV film *Return to Green Acres* a follow-up to her hit sitcom. Her untimely passing in July of 1995 shocked and saddened her many fans who will miss her beauty, wit, and seemingly effortless style and grace.

Current generations seem to hardly know who the Gabors are, let alone who they once were, though the name "Gabor" still brings instant recognition. Quite a few of today's most highly rated shows often find themselves incorporating a "Gabor line" into the script, to guarantee an immediate response and a surefire laugh. You don't get that kind of response from the use of just any name, a point not lost on the writers for such acclaimed television shows as "Will and Grace," "Frasier," "Roseanne," "Home Improvement," "The Larry Sanders Show," and even "Jeopardy," to name just a few. As a matter of fact, going back quite a few years (1958 to be exact) even Rodgers and Hammerstein knew its value and put the name "Zsa Zsa Gabor" into one of their tunes for *Flower Drum Song*. The memorable ditty was "Chop Suey" and the lyrics list all the things that were great about America, from Mickey Mouse to Kennedy,

opposite: Publicity still. Here we see Zsa Zsa in all her bejeweled finery as she lends her "expertise" to an episode of *Dupont Show of the Week* (1962), in a segment appropriately titled "The Beauty of Woman." (Photofest)

top left: Lobby card. Originally released in Europe in 1953 as *Public Enemy Number One*, this amusing farce was rereleased to American moviegoers with the title *The Most Wanted Man* (**Astor**) in 1960.

top right: Though it lacked the punch of other "battle-of-the-sexes" romps of the sixties, *A New Kind of Love* (**Paramount**/1963) did offer Eva the chance to share the screen with real-life husband-and-wife acting team Paul Newman and Joanne Woodward. Set in the world of *haute couture*, this lobby card shows Woodward, Thelma Ritter, George Tobias, and Eva at a fashion show.

middle left: Lobby card from the fun, yet trashy, *Youngblood Hawke* (**Warner Brothers**/1964), based on the Herman Wouk novel. Here we see a pensive Suzanne Pleshette and Eva Gabor vying for the attention of the "naive author-turned-literary sensation," played by James Fransiscus. Pleshette and Eva would become great pals, and would work together again on the 1985 series "Bridges to Cross."

middle right: Lobby card from *Picture Mommy Dead* (**Avco-Embassy**/1966), directed by "horror-meister" Bert I. Gordon. Zsa Zsa portrayed Jessica, the unfaithful wife of star Don Ameche. Zsa Zsa was an eleventh-hour replacement for Hedy Lamarr, who herself replaced Gene Tierney.

bottom left: Lobby card. *Arrivederci, Baby!* (**Paramount**/1966) stars Tony Curtis as a modern-day Bluebeard who marries and murders a succession of global beauties for their money. Zsa Zsa, playing one of the unfortunate brides, is shown here being launched into outer space—never to be heard from again!

bottom right: Suave cat burglar George Hamilton robs Carroll Baker, Lilli Palmer, and Zsa Zsa of their jewels in the frothy film, *Jack of Diamonds* (**MGM**, 1967). The lobby card from this U.S.-German coproduction shows our Hungarian "cupcake" being questioned by a detective, played by Wolfgang Preiss. (All cards Author's collection)

51

The variety show format was the perfect showcase for Eva and Zsa Zsa Gabor, who repeatedly surprised their critics with a dizzying blend of glamour, comedy, *and* music. For more than thirty years both sisters guest starred with practically every major entertainer who hosted a variety program. They lent their support to everyone from Rosemary Clooney to Sha Na Na, and all points in between. Somehow it seemed perfectly natural to see Zsa Zsa performing "High-heeled Sneakers" on "Shindig" or Eva navigating through a sea of giant candelabras while singing "It's So Nice to Have a Man Around the House" on "The Dean Martin Show."

above: Publicity still. Zsa Zsa trips the light fantastic with then-teen sensation Pat Boone on the "Chevy Showroom" in 1960. (Everett)
right: Publicity still. Of the dozens of variety shows and specials on which Eva appeared during the sixties and seventies was "The Beautiful Phyllis Diller Show" in 1968. Here—in Diller "drag"—she clowns around with pal Eddie Albert and the show's star. (AC)

opposite: Publicity still. Zsa Zsa (seen here with Edie Adams) enjoys a light moment of "girl-talk," as the debut guest on the latter's self-titled variety show, in 1963. (Author's collection)

52

to our own indomitable Hungarian Hurricane. Furthermore, her popularity with contemporary humorists, from Rosie O'Donnell to Conan O'Brien, goes to prove that like fine wine, Zsa Zsa (and the Gabor charm) has only improved with age.

Now, Zsa Zsa is left with the task of carrying the "Gabor-aura" into the next millennia, and it shouldn't be too hard. Zsa Zsa has a unique ability to adapt to the everchanging and fickle world of show business; Eva had that talent as well. Each would see their own personas grow and mature with the times. They never waxed nostalgic about Hollywood's "golden years," they simply moved on to new challenges, staying current and active. A Gabor always offered savvy and sophisticated sex appeal, making them quite at home in any decade.

Though Zsa Zsa has been a bit more reclusive of late than her fans would like, no doubt some of the best is yet to come. With a score of talk shows and the popularity of celebrity-driven game shows increasing, the time seems perfect for a host of new Gabor sightings. Her priceless presence is likely to be around for a whole new generation of fans to enjoy. So keep the popcorn buttered, the remote handy, and stay tuned!

WALT DISNEY *presents* The Aristocats — Lost in the Paris countryside, **Duchess** enlists the help of **J. Thomas O'Malley,** cat-about-town.

opposite: Publicity still. *A Nightmare on Elm Street 3: Dream Warriors* (**NewLine**/1987) was the third installment in the amazingly popular horror movie series. Zsa Zsa appears here with a hapless Dick Cavett, beset by a mugging and made-up villian, "Freddy Krueger," played by Robert Englund. (Author's collection)

left: Move over Jane Fonda, it's Zsa Zsa's turn to wear the spandex! Never one to miss an opportunity, Zsa Zsa jumped on the video exercise bandwagon with "It's Simple, Darling!" (1994), and put her own inimitable stamp (with a double-helping of Hollywood beefcake) on the popular craze. (AC)
top: Lobby card. *The Aristocats* (**Disney**/1970) marked Eva's first voiceover for **Disney Studios**, and she would be invited back to "star" in two more of their animated features. (AC)
above: Lobby card. *The Rescuers* (**Disney**/1977) was Eva's second turn at the mike for Disney. Here her character, Miss Bianca, is teamed with that of Bernard (voiced by Bob Newhart). (AC)

55

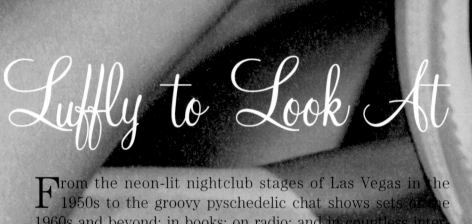

Luffly to Look At

From the neon-lit nightclub stages of Las Vegas in the 1950s to the groovy pyschedelic chat shows sets of the 1960s and beyond; in books; on radio; and in countless interviews around ze vorld, the Gabors have delighted their fans (and playfully tweaked detractors) with delicious *bon mots* for the better part of four decades.

Here is but a sampling of the clever and witty little gems uttered by the first family of feminine pulchritude, peppered within a gallery of their most fetching images.

Caution: You may find yourself freely quoting Gabor*isms* unconsciously to friends and foes alike, but you have been warned. Enjoy!

"If I only had a little humility—I'd be perfect!"

—Zsa Zsa Gabor

"Men are like fires; they go out if left unattended!"

—Zsa Zsa Gabor

previous spread and opposite photo from Author's collection

"I believe in large families: every woman should have at least three husbands."

—Zsa Zsa Gabor

"A man in love is incomplete until he is married; then he is finished."

—Zsa Zsa Gabor

Eva Gabor photo courtesy of Photofest

"There is only one time when you really get to know a man: when you divorce him."

—Zsa Zsa Gabor

"I don't take gifts from perfect strangers—but then, nobody is perfect"

—Zsa Zsa Gabor

"I ask myself more questions than Hamlet as I ponder which shoes to wear."

—Eva Gabor

"How many husbands have I had—you mean apart from my own?"

—Zsa Zsa Gabor

"Fundamentally, the major thing that divides the European male from the American male is the Atlantic Ocean."

—Eva Gabor

"I never hated a man enough to give him his diamonds back."

—Zsa Zsa Gabor

photo from Author's collection

67

"All any girl needs, at any time in history, is simple velvet and basic diamonds."

—Eva Gabor

"I wasn't born, I was ordered from room service."

—Zsa Zsa Gabor

The Magda Mystique

M agda, the most mysterious of the Gabor sisters, was also considered by many as the most naturally beautiful. She had sculpted cheekbones, wavy red hair, exquisitely shaped lips, a becoming figure, and most important, an easygoing ultra-feminine manner. Why then are so few of us even aware of her presence?

It seems as though the spotlight held no special enchantment for the eldest child of Jolie and Vilmos. Where her two siblings ran headlong towards the crowds and flourished, Magda turned and walked away. Possibly it was the financial solvency from her fourth marriage (to Tony Gallucci) that allowed her to settle on a life away from the clamor and chaos of show business. But in this she was not unlike her frequently married sisters, who often found themselves wed to wealthy husbands. However, if the truth be told, Magda too, half-heartedly, attempted to gain acting fame—and, no doubt, she would have recieved it, had she kept at it. Appearing in a small number of theatre productions, radio broadcasts, and television shows she always managed to "steal the show" away from her costars whenever she performed—most notably when she appeared with sisters Eva and Zsa Zsa. Like her more infamous siblings, Magda was not only a natural beauty, but a natural talent and wit as well. Still, this limited success did not convince her to stay an actress; she was not willing to make the sacrifice necessary to become a star. However, in terms of truly unselfish deeds, Magda's were not only charitable, they were life-threatening as well.

Her father, Vilmos, was an army colonel, and Magda inherited his innate sense of social responsibility. However, she chose a most dangerous way to show it. Between 1942 and 1944, Magda was a driver for the International Red Cross. But

opposite: Publicity still. A rare image of Magda "at work," seen here as Nina Dubois from the play *This Thing Called Love.* As short-lived as her professional career was, Magda became emormously popular with theatregoers, because of her easy-going manner and captivating stage presence. But, despite her success which began with a debut on the legitimate stage playing Peggy in *The Women* (1953), Magda quickly grew tired of the "showbiz grind" and left the business by the end of the decade. (Corbis)

above: A beaming Magda, with bouquet in hand, and fourth husband Tony Gallucci, immediately after their 1956 wedding. Proud momma Jolie lends her good wishes at yet another Gabor nuptial. It was, without doubt, Magda's happiest union. The success of the marriage was a strong factor in her decision to abandon her brief foray into acting, and the two remained together until Gallucci's untimely death in 1967 from cancer. (Author's collection)

"To understand her is to understand the flower that closes its petals to the sun; she blooms in private with alluring timidity."

—Jolie Gabor, on her eldest daughter, Magda.

her contribution didn't end there. The cargo she carried was nothing less than neat piles of civilian clothing donated by the Underground. These clothes would be secretly switched for Polish uniforms, thereby helping the soldiers to quietly slip out of Nazi-occupied territory, undetected. This clandestine operation is rumored to have saved more than 5,000 men, and put her life in jeopardy for the duration of the war. Her heroic escape must have also served as added ample fodder for the columnists and journalists to spin their stories once she arrived in America in 1946. But is it any wonder that Magda, before ever setting foot on American soil, would find showbiz a bit false after living through a real life of peril and espionage?

Even into the mid-sixties, after she was struck by a debilitating stroke, Magda mustered the same inner strength as before to fight her way back into life's mainstream. She became an integral part of Palm Springs society and a foundation behind its many charitable organizations. However, the mystery behind her life still remains. To be so close to the edge of supercelebrity, but manage to stay immune from its harsh glare is an amazing feat in itself. But the questions may never be answered; lovely Magda passed away in June 1997, at the age of eighty-one, taking with her her rarely told story.

opposite: Publicity still. Without a doubt, one of the most beautiful images of the eldest Gabor sibling, taken during the mid-fifties. (Corbis)

left: Extremely rare theatre card from the summer stock production of *This Thing Called Love* (1955), a momento from Magda Gabor's brief 1950s acting career. (Author's collection)

above: Magda with Eva and Elsa Schiaparelli, at the couturier's soiree to kick off the 1952 social season. (Corbis)

ROWENA STEVENS
presents
MAGDA GABOR
(IN PERSON)
in
"THIS THING CALLED LOVE"
A SPICY ROMANTIC COMEDY
with
CHARLES G. MARTIN
and a brilliant supporting cast of New York Artists

The lines are terrific and so is GABOR.

Adapted and Directed by
DONALD COOK
Based on the play by EDWIN BURKE
Setting by BALLOU

Magda's professional credits

1950–1953: "The Eva Gabor Show" (WABC Radio); "The Stork Club" with Sherman Billingsley; and numerous other local New York talk shows and personal appearances.

1953: Stage debut in *The Women*; headlined nightclub act with sisters at the Last Frontier Hotel (Las Vegas); costarred with sisters on "The Martha Raye Show" (NBC).

1953–1956: Summer stock productions: *The Play's the Thing; Bernadine; Pajama Tops; This Thing Called Love.*

1955: "Colgate Comedy Hour" (NBC). Appeared with Zsa Zsa, Eva, and Jolie.

Paper Dahlings

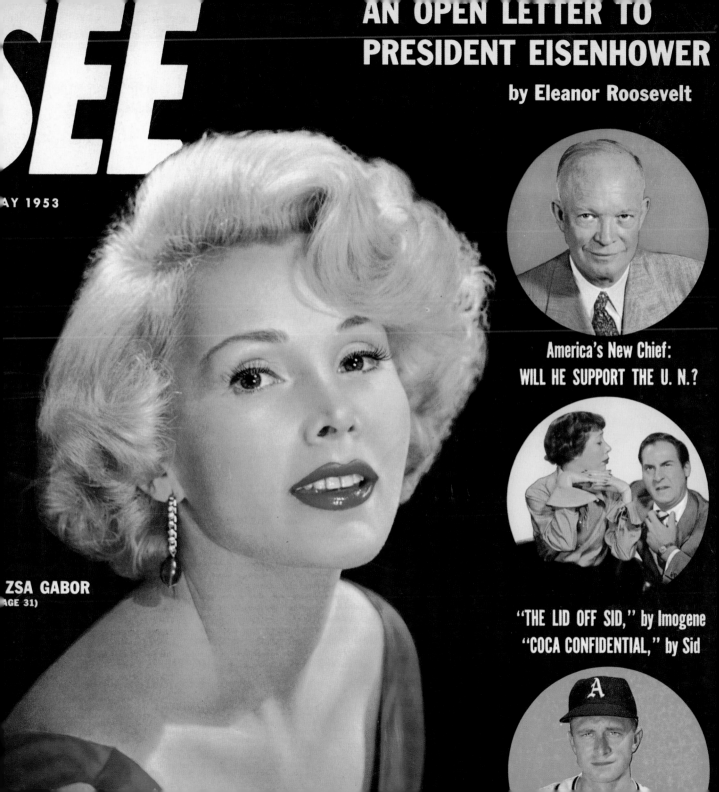

SEE

MAY 1953

ZSA GABOR
(AGE 31)

AN OPEN LETTER TO PRESIDENT EISENHOWER
by Eleanor Roosevelt

America's New Chief:
WILL HE SUPPORT THE U. N.?

"THE LID OFF SID," by Imogene
"COCA CONFIDENTIAL," by Sid

COSMOPOLITAN

September 1950 • 3

CANADA • 40

Eva Gabor

See page 34

Complete Nov

in this Iss

I f the photographs on the previous pages weren't remarkable enough, then in true Gabor fashion, we "gild the lily" by giving further evidence of the Gabors' astounding beauty. Only this time the venue has changed from a collection of glamour portraits to a wide array of national and international magazines. Most are from the midfifties to early sixties, and are stellar examples of their rare beauty. Certainly, without it they could not have had the immediate impact on popular culture that they did. Furthermore, their physical perfection combined with an enormous zeal (and aptitude) for garnering publicity makes the images (and the mystique) all the more memorable.

During the Golden Age of Hollywood, the movie magazine was as important to the success of

previous spread: Zsa Zsa on the cover of **Laff** (American/April 1944), a popular "girlie" magazine of the period. This was probably her first American magazine cover and, interestingly, she was listed as Zsa Zsa Hilton, as she was married to the famed hotel magnate at the time; **Look** (American/June 1952), which also featured cover stories on baseball legend Ty Cobb, and that most ubiquitous fifties threat, flying saucers!; and **See** (American/May 1958), a better "quality" tabloid monthly.

opposite: **Cosmopolitan** (American/Sept. 1950). At the height of her professional success on Broadway, television, and radio, Eva seemed a natural choice as cover girl for what was and is the bible for American career girls.

this page, from top left to right: **Sunday Daily News** (American/June 1952); **Life**, featuring Eva (American/Feb. 1950); **Australasian Post** (Australian/May 1957); **Collier's** (American/Sept. 1952); **Picture Post** (British/Nov. 1952); **This Week**, featuring Eva (American/Nov. 1953); **Pix** (Australian/Oct. 1954); and **Weekend** (British/June 1965). (All Author's collection)

this page, top from left to right: A gathering of "Gabor-clad" German, Dutch, and Austrian magazines, including **ABC** (Dutch/Nov. 1958) with papa Vilmos, sister Madga, and daughter Francesca; **Cliff-Corner** (German/May 1968); **Münchner** (German/Dec. 1954), which shows Zsa Zsa (center) with not only her then-current costar, Gustav Fröhlich (right), from the film *Ball der Nationen*, but also her then real-life leading man, international playboy Porfirio Rubirosa (left); **de Post** (Dutch/Feb. 1954); **Post** (German/July 1953); **Die Neue Illustrietre** (Austrian/Dec. 1954); and **Radio Revue** (German/Feb. 1959).

opposite: **Parade** (American/March 1953). Zsa Zsa found her way onto the cover of this popular supplement to the Sunday news. The magazine amusingly posed the question, "Can Congress use Zsa Zsa Gabor?" If Zsa Zsa's come-hither stare is any indication, the armed forces, CIA, and even the IRS could use her, too. For what man could resist such temptation? (All Author's collection)

a star's career as the films they made. Long before the television talk show, "fan-zines" were a necessary way to promote a motion picture, or for that matter, an up-and-coming actor. Some magazines, from *Screenland* to *Movie Mirror,* boasted monthly cir-cualtions in excess of half a million copies—a sub-stantial figure, indeed. By the early fifties, the public just couldn't get their fill of the "inside stories" on the professional and private lives of their favorite film stars, and editors had more than enough material to keep them satisfied. In these publications the Gabors found themselves featured in a string of silly, studio-engineered articles which almost always found a way to "innocently" drop the name of their "exciting new picture!" *Modern Screen* once proclaimed Zsa Zsa as "the most dan-

parade

Portland Sunday Telegram
Sunday Press Herald

U. S. Citizen 158,676,687 Is Bor

PAGE

Can Congress Use
ZSA-ZSA GABOR

SHOW

THE MAGAZINE OF FILMS AND THE ARTS

ZSA ZSA GABOR
New Sensation on Broadway

**HOLLYWOOD'S
CRAFTSMEN**
Building Everything Under the Sun

TARA IN TOKYO
'Gone with the Wind"
Comes to the Stage

**AMERICAN
FILM INSTITUTE**
Cradle for Young Filmmakers

gerous mantrap since Eve" (whew!) and *Photoplay* tried to titillate us with a "shocking exclusive" about Eva titled, "I Hate to Sleep Alone!" Now I ask you, who wouldn't be profoundly changed by "Zsa Zsa Goes Zshopping" from *TV and Movie Screen,* which followed her to the supermarket for a glimpse into a glamour-girl's grocery list? Heady stuff, huh?

The foreign press also clamored for stories about all of their favorite American film stars. The European markets were enormously important to the studios and they happily obliged. Publications from around the world demanded stories of the stars—some of whom were even more popular abroad. The Gabors most certainly fell into this latter category, especially Zsa Zsa. The fact that she spoke several languages surely didn't hurt,

opposite: Show (American/Aug. 1970), featuring Zsa Zsa during her triumphant Broadway run in *Forty Carats.*

this page, from top left to right: Another cornucopia of Italian, French, and German magazines, featuring our glittering siblings. **Noir et Blanc** (French/Feb. 1953); **Paris Match** (French/Nov. 1961); **Bolero Film** (Italian/Aug. 1953); **Cine Revue** (Italian/March 1958) with Eva; **Cinemonde** (French/Oct. 1953); as testament to their fame in the 1950s, **Visto** (Italian/Jan. 1954) chose to place all three sisters on their cover, following the opening of their Las Vegas nightclub act in 1953; and **Radio Revue** (German/July 1953). (All Author's collection)

this page, from top left to right: A final "smorgasbord" of periodicals. **Wereld-Kroniek** (Dutch/Aug. 1954); **Quick** (German/May 1961); **Le Ore** (Italian/Oct. 1955); **Estudio** (Portuguese/Sept. 1957) with Eva; **L'Europeo** (Italian/1960); **Visto** (Italian/July 1958); **Avondlectuur** (Dutch/1974) with Eva; **Se** (Danish/April 1953); and **De Gouden Ring** (Dutch/1954).

opposite: Zsa Zsa, photographed as Lady Brett Ashley, for the cover of **Cosmopolitan** (American/Aug. 1960). The photo spread also showcased Zsa Zsa in the "roles" of other famous (and infamous) literary heroines that included Sadie Thompson, Lolita, Scarlett O'Hara, and Juliet. (All Author's collection)

and not only were her American films released in international markets, but as early as 1953, she began starring in many European-made pictures. This made her a natural Continental cover girl. She returned the favor by "selling magazines." If Zsa Zsa was considered a "bad girl" by this country's standards, overseas her transgressions were forgiven. Readers were enthralled by perhaps not the "girl next door," but a girl they wouldn't mind living next door to!

Nevertheless, these articles, and especially the images that illustrated them, show that for one brief window in time the Gabors held our attention in rapt and luxuriant splendor. For better or worse, it is a time we will not see again and is an example of how, through beauty, one can forgive all trespasses.

COSMOPOLITAN

ECIAL | August, 1960 • 35¢

FICTION ISSUE

The Sun Is My Shadow

40,000 Word Novel by

Robert Wilder

Author of *Written on the Wind*
and *The Wine of Youth*

The Language
of Love

New French
Movie Girls

ou Can Learn

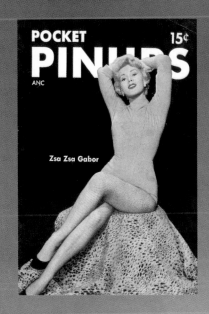

POCKET
PINUPS
ANC
15¢

Zsa Zsa Gabor

Budapest Bombshells

I n their heyday, few women could hold a candle to the pure, unadulterated "femaleness" of a Gabor, and that included all three sisters—Eva, Zsa Zsa, and Magda, and their beautifully zaftig mother, Jolie. From their voluptuous hourglass figures (always tending towards a ripe fleshiness), to the manner and poise with which they carried themselves, the Gabor gals were the perfect physical embodiment of the "softer sex." Coming into full glory during America's most chauvinistic decade, the fifties, only helped in their conquest of the Western world. Interestingly, for all their girlish charm, at the core of each there dwelled the spirit of a fiercely independent thinker. No shrinking violets among this fearless foursome. This unstoppable life force would most readily see itself boil over during one of sister Zsa Zsa's infamous relationships; when she had had enough, it seemed the whole world knew about it. But before any of them became more *fatale* than *femme*, their scantily clad visages managed to grace the pages and covers of many a dime-store adult magazine.

A lot of these periodicals contained legitimate reading matter, but quickly altered their formats (and headline copy) to focus on more salacious content; especially once an ever-expanding audience was discovered for the "taboo" subject matter. Finding its most popular form in convenient pocket-size editions, these "mini-mags" quickly

found their way into the darker recesses of a man's briefcase, bureau, or suit pocket. If you browse carefully through today's newsstand racks, the more brazenly pornographic version of this "quaint" tome is very much alive.

As far as we know, none of the Gabors ever went the distance and took all their clothes off for the camera (or, for that matter, ever appear nude on film). Whether it was due to modesty—not a familiar Gabor trait—or more likely the times in which they became most popular, they were spared that questionable distinction. With that in mind, we were unable to locate a picture of Magda that showed her in a manner any more *provocative* than the one seen here. Prurient pin-up pix of Eva were just as scarce; she always had a wholesome quality to most of her early images and rarely exhibited wanton sexiness. Zsa Zsa, on the other hand, has never been considered camera-shy, and one can only wonder what form her incredibly tame photo spread in *Playboy* (March 1957), featuring her in the Nevada desert wearing the same "gown" as on page 88, would have looked like if photographed with today's relaxed moral standards.

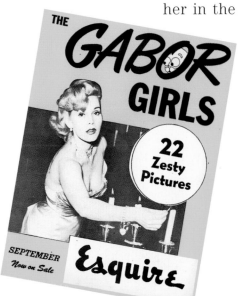

718 ZSA ZSA GABOR—MOVIE STAR © KLM MADE IN U. S. A.

pages 84–85: Publicity still from the mid-fifties. This particular shot was part of a never-ending series of photos featuring Zsa Zsa in clinging, diaphanous gowns intended to provoke and excite the viewer.

opening spread, insert: Rarely did any actress escape "cheesecake" duties, which were largely imposed on them by the studio system as far back as the 1920s. Here we see Zsa Zsa doing her bit for a magazine from 1955 whose name—**Pinups**—certainly speaks for itself. (Author's collection)

previous spread, left: Publicity still. A rare "girlie" shot (c. 1954) of the most enigmatic of the Gabor sisters, Magda. (Everett)

previous spread, bottom left: Newsstand header. This time, for **Coronet**, Zsa Zsa promises to reveal "the men in my life." (Author's collection)

previous spread, bottom right: Newsstand header. Promoting an upcoming issue, this **Esquire** placard playfully teases its male readership with the promise of no less than twenty-two "zesty" pictures of the "Gabor girls." Who could resist!? (Author's collection)

previous spread, right: Publicity still. Eva perches atop a stool in a most abbreviated costume designed to publicize her latest **Metro** release *Don't Go Near the Water* (1957). (Author's collection)

left: "Zsa Zsa Va-Voom!" This undeniably sexy photo from 1957 was used as the header for a promotional calendar, that probably enlivened many a pool hall across the country! (Author's collection)

opposite: A grouping of pocket-size pulp magazines from the fifties through the early sixties, which managed to combine international news and extremely sensational journalism (tame by today's standards) with the prerequisite pretty "dish" on the cover. Certainly, Eva and Zsa Zsa filled the bill nicely as the collection surely indicates. *from top, left to right:* **Ecran** (Chile/1959); **Picture Week** (Amer./1955), Zsa Zsa with daughter Francesca; **Tempo** (Amer./1955) with Eva; **Pulse** (Amer./1954); **Hit Show** (Amer./1961); **Tempo** (Amer./1955); **Picture Week** (Amer./1955); **Quick** (Amer./1952); **Man to Man** (Amer./1957), which featured a cover story entitled "I Left an Arm in Hungary" that, you may be relieved to know, had nothing to do with our cover girl, whose limbs remained intact; **Tempo** (Amer./1953); **Tempo** (Amer./1954); and **People Today** (Amer./1952) with Eva. (All Author's collection)

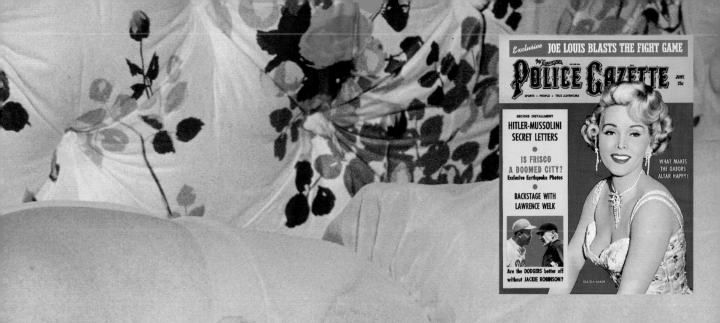

Sugar 'n' Spice

previous spread: Publicity still. An alluring Zsa Zsa welcomes the camera *into her bed* in this titillating fifties candid. (Globe)

previous spread, insert: Not the most auspicious title for a magazine, but **Police Gazette** (American/June 1957) was a popular tabloid of the time, and Zsa Zsa seemed a perfect choice for its cover, which focused on yet *another* exposé of the numerous Gabor marriages. (Author's collection)

above: A rather mean-spirited article accompanies the headline of cheesy mag **Lowdown** (American/1961). (Author's collection)

right: The first and only issue of **Elsa Maxwell's Café Society** magazine (1953). However powerful and influential the famed gossip doyenne was, Maxwell's publication was not successful, thereby making copies of this premiere edition extremely hard to find. (Author's collection)

opposite: Publicity still. Rarely does Eva look as blatantly sexual as she does here in a costume shot from *Paris Model*. Despite some high profile beaus over the years, such as Tyrone Power, Glenn Ford, Ben Gazzara, and even Frank Sinatra, her private life, for the most part, remained that way. Pictures like this one are interesting for the all-too-brief glimpse of Eva's naughtier side, which was usually hidden from prying eyes or eclipsed by the more aggressive Zsa Zsa. (Author's collection)

One can safely assume with a great deal of certainty that women as lovely, magnetic, *and* outspoken as the Gabors never once expected to lead quiet, cautious, and private lives. If anything, it appears to have been the exact opposite. From the very first moment they appeared on the scene they seemed to court all the attention. Certainly momma Jolie herself led a fantastic life, and if she was the example, how could her daughters behave in any less similar a fashion? Inevitably, with all the buzz and bravado came the inevitable ups and downs. In fact, life never was simple for *les femmes Gabor*.

The Gabors are infamous for their riffs and rows—but who's perfect!? Of course Jolie, Magda, and Eva were not saints, but it seems this notoriety most frequently involved lovely Zsa Zsa. If her roles onscreen were often less than stellar, then those moments "off" were *tour de forces*. Yet all the Gabors (including Zsa Zsa) survived the fray quite nicely. Instead of retreating from the prying eye of the public, they met it head on and held their ground. In Zsa Zsa's case, the weight of the charges often leveled against her didn't pull her under; rather than be crippled by unflattering attacks, she seemed to gather strength from the adversity. Over the

Midnight

VOL. 10 — No. 37   MARCH 23, 1964   ★★★ 15¢

ZSA ZSA GABOR'S FORMULA FOR A HAPPY MARRIAGE...

EVERY MAN SHOULD HAVE A MISTRESS

TEENAGE SEX PARTIES
Sensational film expose
PAGE 7

PEOPLE

APRIL 1, 1959   Vol. 10 No. 3

1⁄6

Satellites to change your life
PAGE 38

Zsa Zsa's lament:
WHO CAN AFFORD ME?

HILTON   SANDERS

HAYES   RUBIROSA   TRUJILLO

opposite: Photo still. Her refusal to leave husband George Sanders to marry lover Porfirio Rubirosa sparked a dressing room fracas in Las Vegas, which resulted in a black eye and worldwide publicity. This well-known image, showing Zsa Zsa's infamous eye patch, was picked up by newspapers across the globe. A laughing, "injured" Zsa Zsa is holding a press photo announcing "Rubi's" marriage to Woolworth heiress, Barbara Hutton. Her comment at the time was, "He's Barbara Hutton's problem now, and I wish her the best of luck—she's going to need it!" This would not be the last the world would hear of the saga of Zsa Zsa and Rubi, for his marriage to "Babs" lasted only a mere seventy-three days, thereby allowing him to return to Zsa Zsa, who already "owned" his heart. (Corbis)

Incidentally, the relationship between Zsa Zsa and Rubirosa endured for roughly four years, and surprisingly they never married—although the world assumed that they would. After an abandoned attempt to costar in a film entitled *Western Affair* (1954), the couple went their separate ways but still remained friends. Rubirosa went on to marry nineteen-year-old French model, Odile. The union lasted until an automobile accident—his Ferrari crashed into a chestnut tree on the Bois de Boulogne in Paris—ended the life of the onetime "world's most famous playboy." It was rumored that Rubi's last words were simply, "*Zsa Zsa*"—though she herself doubts the validity of such an absurdly romantic ending.

left, top: The Canadian tabloid, **Midnight** (March 23, 1964), featured a Q & A with the famous bombshell, who expounded once again on her views of life and love. Feminists would have a field day with her "formula" for a happy marriage, but it was no less than one would expect from the queen of questionable quotes! Truly, an interview only Zsa Zsa could give! (Author's collection)

left, bottom: There was no better press agent for Zsa Zsa Gabor than Zsa Zsa Gabor. But at times she could also be her own worst enemy, especially with quotes like, "Who can afford me?" from the Aussie pulp magazine **People** (Australian/1959)—no relation to the current weekly—which is accompanied with a collage of images of beaus, past and present. (Author's collection)

95

above: The scandal-mag **Whisper** (American/Nov. 1958) weighs in on another Zsa Zsa controversy—albeit a tempest in a teapot. As a thank-you for an ultralavish party that she threw for Rafael Trujillo Jr.—the playboy son of Dominican dictator General Trujillo Sr.—she recieved a Mercedes and a chinchilla coat. Unfortunately, the timing for these gifts could not have been worse. At that moment, the United States government was lending financial aid to the impoverished country, and such *largesse* was quickly frowned upon by Congress—which called Zsa Zsa "the most expensive courtesan since Madame de Pompadour." Surprisingly, she was not the only female star to be gifted in this manner—both Kim Novak and Joan Collins were also recipients of expensive presents—however Washington chose to unfairly single her out. Jolie Gabor put all this overreaction into perspective ever so succinctly: "What would you expect a man to send a girl like my daughter, flowers?" (Author's collection)
right: Another sin-sational scandal sheet—**Uncensored** (American/June1954)—which felt it necessary to once again delve into the private life of our *oh so* public Hungarian star. (Author's collection)

opposite: An early sixties "glamour pic" showing a wilder and more aggressive Eva than we were used to seeing at the time. This photo should have come with its own fire extinguisher! (Corbis)

years, Zsa Zsa took great pains to preserve and maintain the glamorous image she fashioned for herself, and if anyone challenged it you had to brace yourself for a mini-Hungarian revolution. Her feuds are legendary, and if you thought they would have been played out away from intrusive eyes, then you would be wrong. A "set-to" might spill out onto the chat show stage, and in a strange bit of performance art, Zsa Zsa positioned herself as writer, director, and star of the tumultuous tableau. But tiffs and tirades aside, even a Gabor had to be shocked by the overwhelming media attention that surrounded Zsa Zsa's cop-slapping trial, in 1989. The end result of this "melodrama" was a three-day jail sentence. Surely no one could have written a more surrealistic latter-day chapter to a life lived in a 24-carat goldfish bowl.

However, when the Gabors were not courting trouble, we get an entirely different picture. They were a hardworking family who, over many decades, labored tirelessly for numerous charitable and humanitarian causes. From Zsa Zsa to Jolie, each one collectively rolled up a chiffon sleeve and pitched in to help. Whatever the need, the Gabors supplied the guts and glamour, which filled the coffers for dozens of worthy organizations.

"*Marriage is too interesting an experiment to be tried only once!*"

—Eva Gabor, on the institution of marriage.

Eat, Drink, and Remarry

Possibly the Gabor women became most infamous for their many marriages *and* divorces. Yet their behavior was not unusual by Hollywood standards, and to their credit, the foursome did not shrink from the bad publicity, but rather wisely incorporated their reputations as altar-happy into their careers. Here is a complete breakdown of their twenty-three trips down the aisle. Phew! That's a lotta rice!

Jolie
Vilmos Gabor, father of Magda, Zsa Zsa, and Eva (1914–1939)
Peter Howard Christman (1947–1948)
Edmund de Szigethy (1957–1989/widowed)

Magda
Count Jan de Bichovsky (1937–39/officially divorced 1946)
William Rankin (1946–1947)
Sidney R. Warren (1949–1950)
Tony Gallucci (1956–1967/widowed)
George Sanders (1970–1971/lasted six weeks)
Tibor Heltai (1972–1973)

Zsa Zsa
Burhan Belge (1937–1941)
Conrad Hilton, father of Francesca (1942–1947)
George Sanders (1949–1954)
Herbert Hunter (1964–1966)
Joshua Cosden, Jr. (1966–1967)
Jack Ryan (1975–1976)
Michael O'Hara (1977–1982)
Felipe de Alba (1982/declared invalid)
Prince Frederick von Anhalt (1986–present)

Eva
Erik Drimmer (1939–1942)
Charles Isaacs (1943–1950)
John E. Williams (1956/divorced within the year)
Richard Brown (1959–1972)
Frank Jameson (1973–1983)

In a darkened movie theatre in 1946, while watching the film *The Moon and Sixpence* starring George Sanders, Zsa Zsa turned to her mother and whispered, "There is my next husband." Within only three years, the little minx was true to her word. She married the suave British actor on April Fool's Day (!) in 1949. Though they would divorce in 1954, they did remain lifelong friends and occasional costars. Years later, Zsa Zsa commented, "Ven I vas married to George Sanders, we were both in love with him. I fell out of love with him, but he didn't." In a bizarre twist, George found his way back into the Gabor family by marrying older sister, Magda. However, the union lasted only six weeks.

opposite: The Sanders' nuptials in Las Vegas on April 1, 1949. In attendance are, from left to right: Allan Shute, Stuart Hall, Jill Lohman, Zsa Zsa, George, William Shiffrin, and Tom Conway (George's brother and best man). (Author's collection)

above: Zsa Zsa and Eva share a happy moment during the wedding reception of sister Magda to Tony Gallucci in 1956. (Author's collection)

Gaborabilia

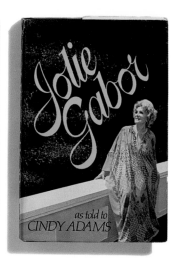

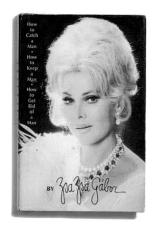

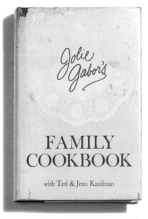

One of the more amusing by-products of celebrity and fame is the inevitable merchandising of the name and image of the star. Some might consider it cashing in, others feel it satisfies consumer demand. Either way, from the very first day that the very first star was "born," there was a manufacturer looming in the shadows with a product to be endorsed. But not everyone can make the grade; like a star on the "Celebrity Walk of Fame," it is an indicator of a celebrity's popularity to be *coveted* so. It is also—depending on the type of association—a mirror that reflects the public's perception of the individual. In the case of the Gabor sisters their images made them perfect for not only ultraglamorous products, but with items that no one would ever associate with Zsa Zsa or Eva. A wonderful example is Zsa Zsa showing us the merits of Lestoil cleaner in 1961. Could you really imagine seeing her use it to scrub the kitchen floor? What do you do with all those diamond rings? That type of juxtaposition between image and endorsement worked beautifully (and comically) when a Gabor was involved.

From perfume to teddy bears, wigs to fake diamonds, cigarettes to khakis, they have all at one time time carried the name Gabor. This in itself is not remarkable; many stars, great and small, have affixed their signatures to far more goods and services. However, the range of clients who engaged them—most often Zsa Zsa—have found that associating themselves with a Gabor gives them an edge on their competitors; one that they couldn't get from just any "run of the mill" celebrity.

With their faces (not to mention their voices) being instantly recognizable, it stood to reason that

previous spread, left: "Zsa Zsa Gabear" was among the numerous celebrity-inspired teddy bears from **The North American Bear Company**, a series that began in the late 1970s. (Author's collection)
previous spread, right top: A gift box assortment of Gabor-endorsed perfumes by L'Argene from the 1950s. Though not Chanel No. 5, the immense popularity of the gals certainly made "scents" to the fragrance industry. (Author's collection)
previous spread, right bottom: Launched in the early seventies, the Eva Gabor International line of wigs (and hair spray) was a successful marriage of beauty and commerce. The synthetic Kanekalon® hairpieces were de rigueur for any "fashionable" woman on the go! Eva was also the company's best advertisement, always wearing one of her own creations. (AC)

opposite, left: Famed illustrator Robert Risko perfectly captures "jailbird" Zsa Zsa Gabor for **Time** magazine, during her sensational cop-slapping trial in 1989. (Courtesy of Robert Risko)
opposite, right, from top left to right: Between the covers: *Orchids and Salami* by Eva Gabor (**Doubleday**, 1954). Eva's autobiography, so titled because friends remarked that those were the only two items ever found in her refrigerator!; *The Jolie Gabor Family Cookbook* by Jolie Gabor with Ted and Jean Kaufman (**Thomas Y. Crowell Company**, 1962). A collection of delectable delicacies from Hungary; *Zsa Zsa Gabor: My Story,* written for me by Gerold Frank (**World Publishing**, 1961). A reflective work on the life of a woman whose career was at a crossroads; *How to Get a Man, How to Keep a Man, and How to Get Rid of a Man* by Zsa Zsa Gabor (**Doubleday**, 1970). A wacky "love guide" for the ladies, as only Zsa Zsa could write; *Jolie Gabor* by Jolie Gabor as told to Cindy Adams (**Mason Charter**, 1975). The often hilarious memoirs of the Gabor grande dame; *One Lifetime Is Not Enough* by Zsa Zsa Gabor with Wendy Leigh (**Delacorte Press**, 1991). The most recent telling of this beauty's sensational life. (All Author's collection)

left: Perfume bottle. "Zig Zag" was introduced by Zsa Zsa Limited in 1969 to great fanfare. Sadly, the fragrance no longer exists, but it would not be Zsa Zsa's last foray in the field. She continued to endorse beauty and skin-care products for many years. (Author's collection)

ZIG ZAG PARFUM

Zsa Zsa and Eva would be natural spokeswomen for a myriad of merchandise beginning in the early 1950s. Over the years, the images of the Gabor sisters have graced numerous print advertisements and television commercials and though this association was not always of the caliber of a Smirnoff or Blackglama, it did show a willingness on their part to compete in the often chaotic world of celebrity "pitch people."

Today, with the mass-marketing of pop culture personalities a rather commonplace occurrence, it would be interesting to see how the sisters—who reached the peak of their notoriety several decades ago—would fare. No doubt, though, with their special talent for attracting attention, they could have given a Madonna or a Michael Jackson a run for the money in the most ubiquitous and outspoken celebrity sweepstakes. Nevertheless, if success is better measured by, as Mark Twain said, "to be spoken of than not spoken of at all," then the Gabors are surely champions without equals.

An assortment of ephemera all dating from the 1950s, including cigarette cards, studio publicity postcards (sent to fans who requested pictures of their favorite stars), and arcade cards. (All Author's collection)

A trio of *Moulin Rouge* memorabilia:

top: A German record on the **Margriet** label.

above: A copy of **Song Hits** (May 1953) "magazine," an odd publication from a time when even the tone-deaf could sing along with their favorite pop tunes.

right: Lenticular. A fun and fascinating novelty from the bygone days of Hollywood promotional items. This three-dimensional framed portrait is lit from within by a lightbulb, and was generally displayed on the walls of theatre lobbies to advertise upcoming films. (All Author's collection)

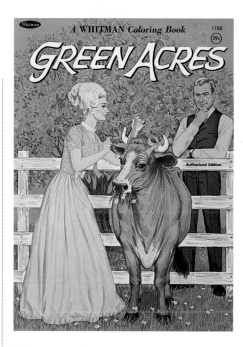

Often memorabilia from popular sitcoms of the past are highly treasured by fans. Such is the case for the wild and zany baby-boomer favorite "Green Acres." Though the show generated fewer pieces of merchandise than many other television shows at the time, individual items are still highly coveted. "Green Acres" related material can go for sky-high prices: a mint condition board game can fetch a whopping $200. For lovers of "Hootervillania," prices for ephemera from Paul Henning–produced shows, including "Petticoat Junction" and "The Beverly Hillbillies," are escalating with no limit in sight. So for those of you who "just adore a penthouse view," happy hunting! "Green Acres" memorabilia also falls into the category of cross-collecting. Individuals who search out "GA" material are not necessarily interested in Eva Gabor—or the reverse. Incidentally, science fiction memorabilia from Zsa Zsa's *Queen of Outer Space* falls into this area, too.

left: A selection of the numerous "tie-in" products for "Green Acres" (1965–71). Included here are the boxed paper dolls (with the Lisa Douglas "standee" and some of her costumes), the board game (which has become increasingly hard to find in the last few years), sheet music of the famous self-titled theme song, and the paper dolls book.
above: The coveted "Green Acres" coloring book. (All Author's collection)

107

The following list, combining those of both Zsa Zsa and Eva, shows as many of the products they endorsed and ad campaigns they were featured in as we were able to verify:

Aamco Transmissions
Ayds Reducing Candies
The Beverly Hills "Break-through" Diet
A Bicentennial Minute
Blackglama Mink
Camel Cigarettes
Canadian Fur Expo
Cadillac Automobiles
Cotts Beverages
Dearfoams Slippers
Draper Clothing
Dreyer's Grand Ice Cream
The Eva Gabor Look, by Estevez
Eva Gabor Interiors
Eva Gabor International Wigs
The Eva Gabor Rose
Ford Motor Company's Ranger
Flemington Furs
Gap Khakis
Greetings From the Stars Audio-cards
L'Argene Fragrances
Lawry's Seasoned Salt
Lestoil Cleanser

Lovejoy Fragrances
Lux Soap
Masterpiece Tobacco
The Men's Tie Foundation
Merv Griffin's Resorts International
Montgomery Ward Auto Club
"No Excuses" Jeans
NutraSweet
Paper-Mate Pens
Pearl de Jolie Cologne
Pearle Vision Centers
Pepsi-Cola
Playtex Undergarments
Rayco Carseat Covers
Riz-Happyli Face Powder
Rubik's Cube
Sarah Coventry Jewelry
Smirnoff Vodka
U.S. Savings Bonds
U.S. Steel
Wheel of Fortune Promo
Whitman Toys
Zsa Zsa Cosmetics, Ltd.
Zsa Zsa Gabor Originals Jewelry

To the left is a collage of some of the original advertisements listed above, including a copy of Eva's endorsement for Blackglama Mink (signed by the star herself!) as well as those for pens, weight-reducing candies, clothing, and a large number for cigarette and alcohol manufacturers—taken during the pre-enlightened forties, fifties, sixties, and seventies.

above: A rather bizarre sampler of perfumes in the form of needle-like vials, marketed by Lovejoy, Inc., with the exotic name "The Book of 7 Secrets." (AC) *right:* A sweetly fragrant still life of the "Gabor family's favorite" scents—or so the label reads—all produced by L'Argene, Inc. If you couldn't look as pretty as a Gabor, you could certainly smell like one! (AC)

Just for fun, coauthor Anthony Turtu wanted to include two of his favorite recipes from the book *Jolie Gabor's Family Cookbook,* by Jolie Gabor, with Ted and Jean Kaufman (Thomas Y. Crowell Company, 1962), for you to whip up at home.

beef goulash with sauerkraut, kende

2	*pounds boneless chuck*
¼	*cup flour*
2	*tablespoons chicken fat*
1	*large onion, minced*
2	*cups soup stock*
½	*teaspoon salt*
½	*teaspoon paprika*
1	*pound sauerkraut, drained*
½	*teaspoon caraway seeds*
1	*tablespoon sugar*
1	*tablespoon lemon juice*
1	*apple, grated*
2	*gingersnaps, softened*
1	*cup sour cream*

Cut meat into 1-inch cubes. Coat evenly with flour. Heat fat in a large pot and brown meat quickly on all sides. Sauté minced onion with meat, adding a little more fat if needed. Add soup stock, salt, and paprika. Bring to a boil and then reduce heat at once. Cook slowly for 2 hours or until meat is fork-tender.

In a separate pot heat sauerkraut, caraway seeds, sugar, lemon juice, and grated apple. Cover and simmer gently for 15 minutes. Soften gingersnaps with 1 tablespoon warm water and blend into meat gravy, stirring constantly until the gravy thickens. Heat sour cream, blend into sauerkraut, simmer gently for a few minutes until all the flavors are blended. Serve with beef goulash. **Serves 6**

golden glazed custard à la Eva

10   egg yolks
¾   cup fine sugar, sifted
1   tablespoon apricot syrup
4   cups rich milk
¼   cup apricot brandy
1   cup preserved chestnuts
      confectioner's sugar

Beat egg yolks together with the sugar and apricot syrup until they are very light and fluffy. Add rich milk and cook slowly in a double boiler until custard coats a spoon. Pour into a sugar-coated, oven-proof pudding dish. Cool. Cover thickly with confectioners' sugar. Place under a preheated broiler, about 6 inches away from heat element, until the top is glazed and golden. Chill thoroughly. **Serves 6 to 8**

This is a delicious custard and was frequently served because of its food value. For best results, cook custard over simmering warm water, stirring constantly until the egg mixture begins to thicken. We had several favorite ways of serving this delicious golden custard. Our cook's specialty was omitting the sugar glaze and serving in its place a most heavenly hot chestnut sauce: heat 1 cup of preserved chestnuts in syrup with ¼ cup of apricot brandy. Serve warm or cold with the chilled soft custard. Timesaving—and delicious.

Both photos courtesy of Globe.

Baubles,
Bangles,
and Leads

If a chronicler of film, television, and stage credits mentioned the Gabors at all, it was often dismissive, and the research cursory at best, providing little insight into the actual scope of their work. We were eager to present as much of a complete listing of their total work as possible. So, for the first time ever, compiled into one book, we give you their professional credits. Roll 'em!

Lovely to Look At (1952)
We're Not Married (1952)
Moulin Rouge (1952)
The Million Dollar Nickel (documentary short/1952)
Lili (1953)
The Story of Three Loves (1953)
El Enemigo Publico No. 1 (French/1953)
Sang et Lumieres (French/1954)
Three Ring Circus (1954)
Ball der Nationen (German/1954)
Western Affair (abandoned project/1954)
Death of a Scoundrel (1956)
Girl in the Kremlin (1957)
The Man Who Wouldn't Talk (British/1957)
Touch of Evil (1958)
Queen of Outer Space (1958)
Country Music Holiday (1958)
For the First Time (1959)
La contessa azzurra (Italian/1959)
Pepe (cameo/1960)
The Road to Hong Kong (unbilled cameo/1962)
Boy's Night Out (1962)
Picture Mommy Dead (1966)
Arriverderci, Baby! (1966)
Mondo Hollywood** (1967)
Jack of Diamonds (1967)
Mooch (TVF, narrator/1971)
Up the Front (British/1972)
Won Ton Ton, The Dog Who Saved Hollywood (1975)
Every Girl Should Have One (1978)
Frankenstein's Great Aunt Tillie (1983–released 1985)
California Girls (TVF/1985)
Dance With a Stranger** (British/1985)
Smart Alec (1986)
A Nightmare on Elm Street 3: Dream Warriors (cameo/1987)
Johann Strauss: The King Without a Crown (1987)

Happily Ever After (voice only/1990)
Naked Gun 2½: The Smell of Fear (cameo/1991)
Blood Ties** (1991)
The Naked Truth (1992)
The Beverly Hillbillies (cameo/1993)
Est & Ouest: les paradis perdus (French/1993)
A Very Brady Sequel (cameo/1996)

Eva on film

New York Town (bit/1941)
Forced Landing (1941)
Star Spangled Rhythm (bit/1942)
Pacific Blackout (1942)
A Royal Scandal (1945)
The Wife of Monte Cristo (1946)
Song of Surrender (1949)
Love Island (1949)
Paris Model (1953)
The Mad Magician (1954)
Captain Kidd and the Slave Girl (1954)
The Last Time I Saw Paris (1954)
Artists and Models (1955)
My Man Godfrey (1957)
Don't Go Near the Water (1957)
Gigi (1958)
The Truth About Women (British/1958)
It Started With a Kiss (1959)
A New Kind of Love (1963)
Youngblood Hawke (1964)
Wake Me When the War Is Over (TVF/1969)
The Aristocats (voice only/1971)
The Rescuers (voice only/1977)
Jack London's Story of the Klondike (ep. Scorn of Women, TVF/1977)
The Nutcracker Fantasy (1980)
Princess Academy (1987)
The Rescuers Down Under (voice only/1990)
Return to Green Acres (TVF/1990)

previous spread: With a sweeping gesture of her velvet stole, Zsa Zsa grandly plays to the camera, while a bemused host, Jack Paar, and an unusually low-key Jayne Mansfield look on, in this photograph from "The Jack Paar Show" from 1962. (Photofest)

opposite: One-sheet poster. British director Herbert Wilcox directed his wife, Dame Anna Neagle, in the taut, little-seen espionage thriller, The Man Who Wouldn't Talk (Lion International/1957). Zsa Zsa, playing a spy, was surprisingly effective in her role opposite Anthony Quayle. (Author's collection)

above: Scene still detail. Though inferior to the 1936 original of the same name, this remake of My Man Godfrey (Universal/1957) did feature fine supporting work by Eva, as Francesca, the sophisticated ex-flame of lead actor David Niven. (Everett)

For pages 114–123:
* Denotes multiple appearances.
**Uncredited appearance, utilizing Zsa Zsa or Eva in either newsreel footage or still photography within the indicated film.
TVF–Indicates a movie specifically made for television or cable.
V–Indicates film made expressly for home video.

Zsa Zsa on stage

1936 (European stage debut)
The Singing Dream (as Violetta, Der Theatre an der Wien, 8/31/36, 100 performances)

1953–1991
Headline nightclub act in various U.S. cities, including:
The Flamingo Hotel • Last Frontier Hotel
The El Rancho Vegas • Riviera Hotel
Las Vegas Hilton • Hotel Tropicana
Las Vegas World (all Las Vegas)
Cafe de Paris (Washington, D.C.)

1956
Sir Lawrence Olivier's "Night of 100 Stars"
(Charity gala, London Palladium; Mistress of Ceremonies)

1958
Pirandello's "A Game for Lovers"
(proposed Broadway debut; abandoned project)

1961–1970 (national tours)
Noel Coward's "Blithe Spirit" (as Elvira)

1970 (Broadway debut)
Forty Carats (as "Anna" Stanley, Aug. 1970, 4 mos., and national tour)

1971–1983 (national summer/winter tours)
Forty Carats • Bell, Book & Candle
Blithe Spirit • Arsenic & Old Lace (with Eva)
Finders Will Return (England)
Ninotchka (title role)

1993
Cinderella (UCLA Theatre Production, as the "Fairy Godmother")

Eva on stage

1943–1949 (local productions, Hollywood, Ca.)
Playtime • The Affairs of Anatol • Candlelight
The Farewell Supper • The Play's the Thing

1950 (Broadway debut)
The Happy Time (Plymouth Theatre, 1/24/50, 18 mos.)

1951–1956 (all national summer/winter tours)
Her Cardboard Lover • The Affairs of State • Candlelight
Blithe Spirit • Strike a Match • Uncle Vanya
Sailor's Delight • Oh Men!, Oh Women!

1956 (Broadway)
Little Glass Clock (John Golden Theatre, 3/26/56, 8 perfs.)

1958 (Broadway)
Present Laughter (Belasco Theatre, 1/27/58, limited run)

1958 (Off-Broadway)
Lulu (Fourth Street Theatre, 9/29/58, 16 perfs.)

1958–1963 (all national summer/winter tours)
Present Laughter • Nude With Violin • The Gazebo • Private Lives
Has Anybody Here Seen Kelly? • Janus • A Shot in the Dark
Critic's Choice • Happiest Man Alive • Blithe Spirit

1963 (Broadway)
Tovarich (10/20/63, limited run/national tour)

1973-1983 (East Coast regional tours)
Blithe Spirit • A Little Night Music
Applause • Arsenic & Old Lace (with Zsa Zsa)

1983 (Broadway)
You Can't Take It With You (Plymouth Theatre, 4/4/83, limited run)

117

above: Scene still from "Rod Serling's Night Gallery" (1971), which gave Zsa Zsa an opportunity to sink her teeth into an unusual character role, and she more than rose to the challenge. As Mrs. Moore, proprietor of a musty thrift shop, Zsa Zsa came into the possession of a "painted mirror" (the episode's title), a deadly and dangerous portal in time. (Author's collection)

opposite: A smattering of fifties, sixties, and seventies regional television guides, from the heartland: Chicago; Pittsburgh; St. Louis; Bloomington, Indiana; and our neighbor to the north: Ottawa, Canada! (AC)

Zsa Zsa on television

1952: RCA Victor Show starring Ezio Pinza; Hope-Crosby Olympic Telethon; Colgate Comedy Hour starring Judy Canova; The Frank Sinatra Show. **1953**: All-Star Revue starring Martha Raye; *The Bob Hope Show (radio); The Martin & Lewis Show (radio). **1954**: The Buick-Berle Show; The Red Skelton Show; The Bob Hope Show. **1955**: Climax (ep. The Great Impersonation); Climax (ep. Man of Taste); The Jack Carson Show; Colgate Comedy Hour starring Martin & Lewis. **1956**: *The Tennessee Ernie Ford Show; The Milton Berle Show; The Ford Show; The Herb Shriner Show; The Ernie Kovacs Show; The Jack Benny Show; Screen Gems; G.E. Theatre (ep. The Honest Man); Matinee Theatre (ep. The Tall Dark Stranger); Climax (ep. The Louella Parsons Story); Ford Theatre (ep. Autumn Fever); Matinee Theatre (ep. The Babylonian Heart); Just Plain Folks (pilot); Love That Bob (ep. Grandpa Meets Zsa Zsa). **1957**: Playhouse 90 (ep. The Greer Case); Playhouse 90 (ep. Circle of the Day); Matinee Theatre (ep. The Last Voyage); *The Arthur Murray Dance Party; The Rosemary Clooney Show; The George Gobel Show; The Life of Riley (ep. Foreign Intrigue); *The Dinah Shore Chevy Show. **1958**: Shower of Stars; Matinee Theatre (ep. The Europeans); The Jack Benny Program; 30th Annual Academy Awards; Matinee Theatre (ep. The Subpoena); Matinee Theatre (ep. The Two Mrs. Carrolls). **1959**: Lux Playhouse (ep. This Will Do Nicely); December Bride (ep. The Zsa Zsa Gabor Show); The Bob Hope Special; Kraft Music Hall; The Bob Hope Buick Show. **1960**: The Pat Boone Chevy Showroom; Love Is a Funny Thing; Special Tonight (ep. Ninotchka): Danny Thomas Show (ep. Kathy and the Glamour Girl). **1961**: Candid Camera; The Bob Hope Show; G.E. Theatre (ep. The Legend That Walks Like a Man); The Bob Hope Buick Christmas Show; Saturday Night at the Movies (narrator, Riviera travelogue). **1962:** Dupont Show of the Week (ep. The Beauty of Woman) **1963:** The Edie Adams Show; Dick Powell Show (ep. Charlie's Duet); Mr. Ed (ep. Zsa Zsa); Burke's Law (ep. Who Killed Cable Roberts?). **1964**: Joey Bishop Show (ep. Redecorating the Nursery); Burke's Law (ep. Who Killed Super Sleuth?). **1965**: Bob Hope Chrysler Theatre (ep. Double Jeopardy); Gilligan's Island (ep. Erika Tiffany Smith to the Rescue); Shindig. **1966**: F Troop (ep. Play, Gypsy, Play); Alice in Wonderland (voice only); The Rounders; The Sammy Davis, Jr. Show. **1967**: Bonanza (ep. Maestro Hoss); The Dom DeLuise Show. **1968**: *Rowan & Martin's Laugh-In; A Special for Bob Hope; My Three Sons (ep. Ernie and Zsa Zsa); Batman (ep. Minerva, Mayhem and

Millionaires); Name of the Game (ep. Fear of High Places). **1969**: The John Gary Show; Bracken's World (ep. King David). **1970**: The Bob Hope Special. **1971**: Bob Hope's 22nd Anniversary Special; The 13th Annual Grammy Awards; Night Gallery (ep. The Painted Mirror). **1972**: Flood Relief Special starring Bob Hope. **1973**: The Flip Wilson Show; *The Dean Martin Comedy Hour. **1974**: The Bluffers; *The Dean Martin Celebrity Roasts; Bob Hope's Las Vegas Entertainment Awards; Wide World of Entertainment. **1975**: Bob Hope's Cavalcade of Champions; Texaco Presents: Highlights of a Quarter Century of Bob Hope Specials; The Noonday Show. **1976**: Texaco Presents: Bob Hope's World of Comedy. **1977**: Sha-Na-Na; 3 Girls 3. **1978**: "Happy Birthday, Bob!" **1979**: Supertrain (ep. A Very Formal Heist). **1980**: The Love Boat (ep. Return of the Captain's Brother); Men Who Rate a Ten; The 15th Annual Academy of Country Music Awards; Bob Hope's Overseas Christmas Tours. **1981**: The Facts of Life (ep. Blair and the Countess); *As the World Turns (serial, several episodes); The All-Star Salute to Mother's Day (with Eva). **1982**: Bob Hope's "Women I Love–Beautiful But Funny"; Texaco Star Theatre: Opening Night; Today Show (Epcot Center opening); Knots Landing (ep. Svengali). **1983**: Matt Houston (ep. The Purrfect Crime); The AFI Salute to John Huston; I Love Men; Mario Lanza: The American Caruso. **1984**: Foul-Ups, Bleeps and Blunders; TV's Bloopers and Practical Jokes; Dom DeLuise and Friends II; Circus of the Stars (Germany). **1985**: The Start of Something Big; The Soap Opera Digest Awards; The Nosotros/Golden Eagle Awards. **1987**: Charlie Barnett's "Terms of Enrollment" (V); It's Garry Shandling's Show; The Marital Bliss Telethon (hostess). **1988**: The Munsters Today; Stars of the Century (V); Pee Wee's Playhouse Christmas Special. **1989**: Hollywood on Horses (V); "Europa, Europa"; Miss Hollywood Talent Search. **1990**: City. **1991**: The Fresh Prince of Bel Air. **1992**: Prime Time Live (seg. A Day in the Life of Hollywood); Evening at the Improv (hostess); Civil Wars; Empty Nest. **1994**: David Letterman's Late Show Video Special. **1995**: Cybill; Four Weddings and Zsa Zsa (hostess); **2000:** The 70s: The Decade That Changed Television.**; A&E's Biography: The Gabors; National Enquirer Uncovered.**

Eva on television

1949: Your Show Time (ep. A Lodging for the Night); Silver Theatre (ep. L'Amour the Merrier); Studio One (ep. At Mrs. Beam's). **1950**: The March of Dimes Fashion Show; Masterpiece Playhouse (ep. Uncle Vanya);

above: A sixties fan postcard of a deliciously playful Eva, which features a stamped signature on back. (Author's collection)

Showtime USA. **1951**: Your Show of Shows; The Kate Smith Hour (ep. The Game); Sister Kenny Foundation Telethon; The Kate Smith Hour (ep. Incident in Paris); Coast Guard Cadets on Parade (radio); The Mel Torme Show; Famous Women of History with Eva Gabor; The Stork Club Show; Story Theater (ep. Lodging for the Night); Suspense (ep. This Is Your Confession); Ellery Queen (ep. Adventures of the Twilight Zone); Tales of Tomorrow (ep. The Invaders). **1952**: Texaco Star Theatre; *The Bob Hope Show (radio); Pulitzer Prize Playhouse (ep. Return of Mr. Moto). **1953**: All-Star Revue with Martha Raye; Philco Theater Playhouse (ep. The Gesture); Suspense (ep. The Duel). **1954**: *The Arthur Murray Dance Party; Studio One (ep. Paul's Apartment); The Easter Parade of Stars; Justice (ep. The Blackmailer). **1955**: The Colgate Comedy Hour; Pond's Theater (ep. Candle Light); Way of the World; Justice (ep. The Intruder); Appointment with Adventure (ep. Notorious Woman); Philco Television Playhouse (ep. One Mummy Too Many); Kraft Theater (ep. Once a Genius). **1956**: Kraft Theater (ep. Ten Grapefruit to Lisbon); The Tennessee Ernie Ford Show; Matinee Theater (ep. Pearls of Sheba); Climax (ep. Journey Into Fear); Tales of the 77th Bengal Lancers (ep. Steel Bracelet). **1957**: G.E. Theater (ep. The Big Shooter); Climax (ep. Jacob and the Angel). **1958**: Matinee Theater (ep. The Vagabond); G.E. Theater (ep. Ah There, Beau Brummel); Matinee Theater (ep. Nine-Finger Jack); Further Adventures of Ellery Queen (ep. So Rich, So Lonely, So Dead). **1959**: The Big Party for Revlon; Five Fingers (ep. Station Break); Adventures in Paradise (ep. Peril at Pitcairn). **1960**: U.S. Steel Hour (ep. How to Make a Killing); The Detectives (ep. The Retirement of Maria Muir); Ann Sothern Show (ep. Katy and the New Girl); Dow Hour of Great Mysteries (ep. The Great Impersonation); Harrigan and Son (ep. There's No Fool Like an Old Fool). **1961**: Harrigan and Son (ep. They Were All in Step but Jim); Ann Sothern Show (ep. The Royal Visit); Dick Powell Show (ep. The Fifth Caller); The Defenders (ep. Gideon's Follies). **1962**: U.S. Steel Hour (ep. Two Black Kings). **1963**: Mickey and the Contessa (pilot); Burke's Law (ep. Who Killed Harris Crown?). **1965**: Green Acres (series to 1971); Petticoat Junction (eps. The Baffling Raffle; Bobbie Jo's Sorority; The Good Luck Ring; Joe Carson, General Contractor; Hooterville A Go-Go; Betty Jo Goes to New York; The Young Matchmakers). **1966:** Petticoat Junction (Yogurt, Anyone?). **1967**: The 19th Annual Emmy Awards; Coliseum (hostess); The 15th Annual International Beauty Pageant (hostess).The Smothers Brothers Comedy Hour. **1968**: The Beautiful Phyllis

Diller Show; The 20th Annual Emmy Awards; Petticoat Junction (ep. The Valley Has a Baby); The Beverly Hillbillies (ep. The Thanksgiving Story); Petticoat Junction (ep. Wings); Here's Lucy (ep. Lucy and Eva Gabor). **1969**: *The Dean Martin Show; The Liberace Show; Howdy (pilot); Petticoat Junction (ep. The Ballad of the Everyday Housewife). **1970**: The Tennesssee Ernie Ford Special; The Kraft Music Hall; The Pat Paulsen 1/2 Comedy Hour; The 22nd Annual Emmy Awards; Wonderful World of Disney (ep. From All of Us to All of You). **1971**: The Red Skelton Show; The Jim Nabors Show. **1972**: The Bob Hope Comedy Special; Ken Berry's WOW Show; Here's Lucy (ep. Lucy and Eva, Hospital Roommates). **1973**: The Wacky World of Jonathan Winters. **1974**: Wide World of Entertainment. **1975**: Bob Hope's Cavalcade of Champions; Big Eddie; Ellery Queen (ep. The Adventure of the Blunt Instrument). **1976**: Bob Hope's World of Comedy. **1977**: Rosetti and Ryan (ep. Ms. Bluebeard); The Love Boat (ep. Dear Beverly). **1978**: CBS, On the Air; Wonderful World of Disney (ep. Mickey's 50th); The Comedy Shop; Fantasy Island (ep. Widow); Almost Heaven (pilot). **1981**: All-Star Salute to Mother's Day; Fantasy Island (ep. The World's Most Desirable Woman). **1982**: Madame's Place; Night of a Hundred Stars (special); The Love Boat (ep. Mother's Don't Do That); Hart to Hart (ep. With This Hart, I Thee Wed). **1983**: Edge of Night (serial). **1984**: All-Star Party for Lucille Ball; TV's Bloopers and Practical Jokes; Hotel (ep. Prisms). **1986**: The Love Boat (ep. The Prediction); Bridges to Cross (series). **1987**: She's the Sheriff (ep. Butterfly Is Free). **1988:** The American Image Awards (hostess) **1989**: The Gregory Harrison Show (pilot). **1990**: Close Encounters (pilot). **1991**: Merv Griffin's New Year's Eve Special; Dream On. **1992**: Hi Honey, I'm Home! **1993**: The Legend of the Beverly Hillbillies (special). **1994:** Burke's Law (ep. Who Killed Romeo?). **1998**: Intimate Portrait (posthumous subject). **2000:** A&E's Biography: The Gabors.

Zsa Zsa on quiz, talk, panel shows, and newsmagazines

1951–52: Bachelor's Haven. **1953**: I've Got a Secret; Place the Face; Who Said That?; *What's My Line?; This Is Show Business. **1954**: *Tonight Show starring Steve Allen; The Name's the Same. **1955**: The Sheilah Graham Show. **1956**: The Johnny Carson Show; Masquerade Party; Nightbeat; *The Steve Allen Show; *The Walter Winchell Show; *It Could Be You; *Truth or Consequences. **1957**: Tonight! After Dark. **1958**: *Tonight Show starring

above: A late eighties candid of Zsa Zsa, being interviewed for "Entertainment Tonight." In addition to being a frequent guest on chat shows, Zsa Zsa was also a consistent presence on numerous newsmagazines—as either an interviewee or subject. (Noble/Globe)

above: Perennial television favorite Zsa Zsa mugs for the photographers on the set of "Art Linkletter's House Party" in 1959, with her pet yorkie, Mr. Magoo. The pooch was a small screen regular who accompanied his mistress on scores of other shows. (Sid Avery/MPTV)

Unbeknownst to many, Zsa Zsa was a devoted animal lover and cared for dozens of them over the years. Some of her more cherished furried and feathered companions have included: Lady, a German shepherd, and Elizabeth, a canary, both childhood pets; Mishka, a Scottie; Fatushka, an Arabian horse; Canum, a mutt she rescued while living in Turkey; Harem, another horse; Caesar, a Macaw, who had a rather salty mouth and would hurl expletives at anyone who entered the room; Mimi, her beloved poodle (seen on page iv); Harvey Hilton, another pampered poodle; Suzie, a photogenic Yorkie; Miss Pussycat, a longhaired Persian; a host of Shih-Tzus (favorites with all the Gabors) including Zoltan, Genghis Khan, Macho Man, Pasha Effendi, and Genghis Khan II; King, another well-loved German shepherd; and Silver Fox, Zsa Zsa's pride and joy Tennessee Walker, whom she had the honor of riding at the opening ceremonies for the 1984 Los Angeles Olympics.

Jack Paar; Mike Wallace Interviews. **1959**: You Asked for It; Dick Clark's World of Talent; Take a Good Look; Art Linkletter's House Party; Person to Person; The Hobby Lobby. **1960**: *Play Your Hunch; This Is Zsa Zsa (radio). **1961**: The Today Show (with Dave Garroway). **1962**: Talent Scouts; *Tonight Show (var. hosts); Here's Hollywood; *Your First Impression. **1963**: *Girl Talk; *Tonight Show starring Johnny Carson. **1964:** The Celebrity Game; The Regis Philbin Show; *The Jack Paar Program. **1965**: *The Eamonn Andrews Show (England); Front Page Challenge (Canada); The Pamela Mason Show. **1966**: *Hollywood Squares; *The Merv Griffin Show; The Bruce Forsyth Show (England). **1967**: *Personality; Everybody's Talking; Celebrity Billiards; *The Dating Game; *The Joey Bishop Show; Good Company. **1968**: *Kup's Show; The Weaker Sex; Funny You Should Ask; The Jerry Lewis Show; Here Come the Stars; The Diana Dors Show (England, pilot). **1969**: Name Droppers; Playboy After Dark; *The David Frost Show. **1970**: *Letters to Laugh-In; The Mike Douglas Show; For Women Today; Can You Top This? **1971**: Juvenile Jury; The Virginia Graham Show. **1972**: *Dinah's Place; Midday Live (NY only). **1973**: Hollywood's Talking. **1974**: *Dinah! **1975**: Don Adam's Screen Test; Sammy & Company; Let's Make a Deal. **1976**: *Tattletale's; Talking Pictures (pilot); *Break the Bank; Crosswits. **1977**: *Hollywood Connection. **1978**: The $1.98 Beauty Show; PM Magazine; When Havoc Struck. **1979**: Dance Fever; All-Star Secrets. **1980**: The John Davidson Show. **1981**: Over Easy. **1982**: Fantasy; The Regis Philbin Show; The Today Show; Sportsworld. **1983**: NBC News Overnight; Thicke of the Night; F. Lee Bailey's Lie Detector. **1985**: Lifestyles of the Rich and Famous; Barbara Woodhouse in Beverly Hills. **1986:** Steve Allen: All the Best (V) **1987**: The Dame Edna Experience (England); Ask Dr. Ruth; The Morning Program; *Animal Crack-Ups. **1988**: The Late Show with Ross Shafer; The Morning Show. **1989**: The People Vs. Zsa Zsa Gabor (unauthorized video); Live at Five; *The New Hollywood Squares; *Entertainment Tonight; The Pat Sajak Show; *The Home Show; *Larry King Live; The Oprah Winfrey Show; *The Phil Donahue Show; *The Joan Rivers Show; Sally Jessy Raphael; *The Marsha Warfield Show; *Joan Lunden's Everyday; *The Arsenio Hall Show; Un Dia es un Dia (Spain). **1990**: *Geraldo; *Hard Copy; Personalities; *Into the Night. **1991**: One on One with John Tesh; The Full Wax (England); The Mark Simone Show (radio); Late Nite with David Letterman; Johnny B. On the Loose. **1992**: *The Maury Povich Show; New York Nights; The Thomas Gottschalk Show (Germany); Attitudes; Christina; *The Howard Stern Show. **1993**:

*Vicki! **1994**: Extra!; The Clive James Show (England); The Late Show with David Letterman; Late Night with Conan O'Brien; The Ricki Lake Show; It's Simple, Darling (V). **1997**: The Ruby Wax Show; The Rosie O'Donnell Show.

Eva on quiz, talk, panel shows, and newsmagazines

1950: Answer Yes or No; Fifteen with Faye; *Leave It to the Girls. **1950–51**: The Eva Gabor Show. **1951**: Footlights and Klieglights; The Steve Allen Show; *This Is Show Business; Quick on the Draw. **1952**: The Eve Hunter Show; *The Walter Winchell Show. **1953**: Quick As a Flash (debut guest); The Name's the Same; *The Big Payoff. **1954**: *The Today Show; On Your Way; *What's My Line; Droodles; The Betty White Show. **1955**: *The Tonight Show starring Steve Allen; The Ted Mack Matinee. **1956**: *Truth or Consequences; *It Could Be You. **1957**: *The Tonight Show starring Jack Paar; The Arlene Francis Show. **1958**: You Asked for It. **1959**: I've Got a Secret; Dick Clark's World of Talent. **1960**: Here's Hollywood; Person to Person; Masquerade Party. **1962**: *The Tonight Show (various hosts); The Merv Griffin Show (NBC daytime); *The Tonight Show starring Johnny Carson; *Girl Talk (debut guest); Your First Impression. **1963**: The Object Is; *The Jack Paar Program **1964**: *Password; Missing Links. **1967**: *Personality; *The Joey Bishop Show; *The Mike Douglas Show; *Hollywood Squares (NBC daytime). **1968**: *Kup's Show (syn.). **1969**: It Takes Two. **1970**: Life with Linkletter; *TheEamonn Andrews Show (England). **1971**: The Virginia Graham Show. **1972**: Jerry Visits; *Dinah's Place; *The Merv Griffin Show (syn.). **1973**: *Hollywood Squares (syn.). **1975**: *Tattletales. **1976**: Take My Advice. **1977**: The Eva Gabor Specials (syn.); *The Gong Show. **1978**: The Cheap Show. **1979**: *Match Game PM; Mindreaders; All-Star Secrets; Dance Fever. **1981**: *The Match Game. **1984**: Good Sex with Dr. Ruth; Late Night with David Letterman. **1985**: Hour Magazine. **1986**; Beverly Sassoon's Total Beauty (V). **1988**: The New Hollywood Squares; Regis Philbin's Lifestyles. **1989**: *Entertainment Tonight; Lifestyles of the Rich and Famous; Alive and Well; Attitudes. **1990**: *Live at Five; Live with Regis and Kathie Lee; Celebrity Chefs. **1991**: CNN Showbiz Today; *The Home Show; The Joan Rivers Show; *The Arsenio Hall Show; Runaway with the Rich and Famous. **1992**: New York Nights; One on One with John Tesh; Vicki!. **1994**: Marilu. **1995**: Geraldo.

above: It takes two to tango, as we see here in a lighthearted moment from "The Mike Douglas Show," where Eva was a frequent and popular guest. Like Zsa Zsa, Eva was a talk show favorite, whose turns "on the couch" were always glamorous, witty, and serene—*unlike* appearances by her unpredictable sister, who could always be counted on for her own brand of fireworks. (Everett)

The Gabors' lives have taken them from the sun-drenched sands of the Riviera to the cherry blossom–scented streets of Tokyo; from the chalets of the Swiss Alps to the mansions of Bel-Air, and everywhere in between. They have worked with everyone from a glitzy Liberace to a ditzy Pee Wee Herman; from *bon vivant* Noël Coward to the incorrigible Smothers Brothers; from the Great White Way's David Merrick to rap sensation Will Smith; from Vincente Minnelli in Hollywood to the Beatles at the London Palladium. They traded quips and barbs with funnymen Bob Hope, Milton Berle, and Red Skelton to Garry Shandling, David Letterman, and Howard Stern. Famed animators Chuck Jones and Matt Groening both used them as comic muses for their work. They were gowned by Christian Dior and Cecil Beaton in the fifties and served as inspiration for Claude Montana more than thirty years later. Great photographers from Avedon to Annie Leibovitz recorded them for posterity. They were "roasted" by Dean Martin and toasted by presidents. From El Morocco to Studio 54, they were there—and luckily, they took us along for the ride.

Gaborabilia is an homage to these "vonderful vimmen," who were sometimes irrationally judged, harshly criticized, and unfairly dismissed; but who, through drive, humor, style, and yes, talent, helped us all see things a little more glamorously and a little less seriously. For this, we should all be grateful.

opposite: If this brilliant Valentine-red portrait of Zsa Zsa doesn't take your breath away, then you're already dead, sweetheart! Simply stated, it's perfection. (Wallace Seawell/MPTV)

below: Publicity still. Eva in a strapless chiffon confection, looking long, lean, and lithe during her tenure at Metro-Goldwyn-Mayer in the late fifties. (Author's collection)

following spread: Zsa Zsa assumes a can-can–inspired pose in a sumptuous black velvet strapless. (Kobal)

page 128: A final grouping of coauthor Anthony Turtu's many Gabor portraits.

Afterword

acknowledgments

This labor of love would not have been possible without the help and support of numerous friends, individuals, and organizations. The authors would like to thank the following—*a list that reads as diversely as the guests on a sixties chat show!*:

To everyone at Three Rivers Press—especially Doug Pepper, David Tran, and Tim Roethgen—for their hard work and enthusiasm on our behalf. To Robert, Frank and Theresa Turtu, the Reuters, Tom, Joe and Dan, Kevyn, Denis, Geoffrey Beene, Joyce, Peter and John, Teresa and Ward, Miisa and Lee, Darlene and John, Mitch and Harris, Jim and Gary, Mark, Frank, Wayne, Red and Smokey; to Norman Curry and Donna Daley at Corbis; Howard Mendelbaum and crew at Photofest; Bob Cosenza at Kobal; Todd Oldham; Meryl Rodney and Glen Bradie at Everett; Janice Silver; Jim Walsh; RuPaul Charles; Yen Graney at MPTV; Globe Photos, John Cocchi at JC Archives; Mr. Blackwell; Rocky Pilero; Peter Rogers; Robert Risko; Susan Benson; Jean Osta; Bruce Stapleton, Tina Hummel; Steve Hanson at UCLA Film Archives; Donna Holden of Hatos-Hall Productions; Jess Morgan & Company; Julie Hirsch of Dick Clark Productions; Peg Barry; Jules Power; RoseMarie; Fred Wostbrock; David Schwartz; Comzone; Pierre Cossette Productions; Charles Connelly; Roberto Diaz; Allene Arthur; and Phyllis Diller.

Extra special kudos to Billy Jim for his amazing still-life photography, which transformed a series of inanimate objects into miniature works of art.

And most especially to the late Mr. Steve Allen, who took time from *his* many endeavors, to bring learned perspective and clarity to *ours*. Thank you, Steverino, it was truly an honor!

viszontlatasra

*dahlings!**

*Till we meet again, in Hungarian